DINING IN—BOSTON

Steven Raichlen
Foreword by Sheryl Julian

PEANUT BUTTER PUBLISHING
Peanut Butter Towers   Seattle, Washington   98134

OTHER TITLES IN SERIES:

Cover photo by M. Skott/Image Bank West

CONTENTS

In much the same way that Parisians once looked down upon the cooking of the various regions throughout France as not being sophisticated enough, Boston has been denounced by its New York neighbors as being part of the provinces. Bostonians have been typed as being frugal, unadventurous and gastronomically uneducated, and to add insult to injury, the city has suffered because it's the last stop for transport trucks delivering vegetables and fruits from Florida and California.

But as Boston itself has changed drastically over the last fifteen years, so have the attitudes toward Bostonians and their restaurants. To discover the physical differences in the city, one has only to drive along the Charles River and see the mirror-covered John Hancock Tower, reflecting all the other buildings around it; or to wander along the newly renovated waterfront or through the food stalls and shops of downtown's Faneuil Hall Marketplace. Everywhere that the new buildings have been built, or old ones uncovered, restaurants have appeared shortly afterward. The people have changed, the city is different and dining out in Boston is a reflection of all of that. Although Boston will always be the last stop for the transport trucks driving north or east, it is the first stop for the fishing vessels carrying the impressive catch of the coastline. Local farming is endorsed and encouraged by government agencies and everyone has rallied to support the young innovative chefs who have helped prove how responsive Bostonians really can be.

The city's restaurants offer something for everyone: hotel dining rooms which serve in the old tradition; large seafood houses which offer local fish and shellfish and familiar New England seafood specialties; small adventurous bistros where the dishes change as often as the chef's whims; international cuisine from the Orient, to Africa, to Europe; and formal classic restaurants which are trustworthy and dependable no matter how much the skyline around them varies.

Boston has finally come into its own and the facets of its personality are mirrored on its tables. The dining rooms of the Colonnade, Parker House and the Copley Plaza are as stately as one would expect from a Boston hotel. Maison Robert, the classic French restaurant housed in Boston's Old City Hall, is presided over with dignity by its admired chef and owner, Lucien Robert. And the young chefs—at the Voyagers, L'Espalier, the Harvest, Cybele's, Felix Krull, Panache, Le Bocage and

Allegro—are energetic, enthusiastic, thoughtful, clever and talented.

Despite what our neighbors to the west might say when they compare their restaurants to ours, we have several advantages over them, not the least of which is this: Boston is not only a nice place to visit, it's a wonderful place to live as well.

Sheryl Julian

PREFACE

When I first moved to Boston, I was warned that if I wanted to eat well, I would have to learn how to cook for myself. Implied by the advice, I suppose, was that Boston was not a dine-out city, at least not one with the variety and stature of my previous domicile—Paris. As I had come to New England to teach cooking classes, I was not particularly worried by the warning.

It was not long, however, before I began to discover just the contrary—that Boston's restaurants had a lot to offer, and not just to a cooking teacher who, from time to time, tired of his own cooking. There is great seafood in Boston—a bounty found in few other American cities—supplied by the fish-rich waters of the North Atlantic. There is also, in this oldest of American cities, a long and continuous tradition of fine dining, including a handful of restaurants that opened their doors to the public more than a century ago. I soon came to meet the many faces of ethnic Boston, whose Oriental, Italian and Slavic communities dish up their exotic specialties in marvelous profusion. I arrived in this city of gold domes and tall church spires just in time to witness the birth of a veritable culinary revolution, led by bright young chefs who drew their inspiration from French nouvelle cuisine and their ingredients from the comestible cornucopia of New England.

The research and writing of *Dining In—Boston* has been an adventure of culinary discovery for me. What better way to learn about cooking than to meet and talk to the chefs of Boston's twenty-one top restaurants? These remarkable cooks have generously shared not only their prized recipes, but also their hard-earned kitchen wisdom. It is with great pleasure and excitement that I pass on the secrets of their specialties to the readers of *Dining In—Boston*.

"A recipe is like a score of music," remarked one of the chefs I interviewed. I think the analogy is worth pursuing. Anyone with the barest musical training can hammer out note by note the score of a Brandenburg concerto. Let a true musician bring but a little sensitivity, improvisation and feeling to the piece, and the audience will weep for joy when it hears the performance. So it is with cooking. A teaspoon by teaspoon rendition of a recipe never produced a culinary masterpiece. Add a dash of inspiration, a pinch of folly, a splash of love to the recipes in *Dining In—Boston*—as do the chefs who prepare these dishes in their restaurants —and you will wind up with food that makes beautiful music.

Discover the taste of Boston, then, with the talented men and women chefs who make it possible. From all of us, happy cooking. And, *bien sûr, bon appétit!*

Steven Raichlen

ABOUT THE AUTHOR

Steven Raichlen has always had a literary love affair with cooking. As a student at Reed College in Portland, Oregon, he majored in French literature, working between semesters at a gourmet delicatessen which made all its own sausage on the premises. Upon graduation in 1975, he received a Thomas J. Watson Foundation Fellowship for a year-long study of medieval cooking in Europe.

So Raichlen packed off to Paris to discover long-lost techniques amid the dusty shelves of Europe's great libraries. He acquired his practical culinary skills first at the Cordon Bleu, then at the newly opened Ecole de Cuisine La Varenne. Fluent in French, Raichlen was one of La Varenne's first stagiaires, where his foreign-language skills were put to good use in translating the school's cooking demonstrations. At the same time, under the tutelage of Chef Fernand Chambrette, he widened his understanding and expertise in classical haute cuisine. More recently, Raichlen completed a summer-long stint in Brittany at the Michelin-starred restaurant of rising young Chef Louis LeRoy, where he gained hands-on experience in the exacting, precise preparation of such nouvelle cuisine specialties as lobster en papillote and monkfish with raspberries.

On his return to the United States, Raichlen embarked on a career in food journalism. He writes a monthly food and drink column for *Boston Magazine*. His articles have appeared nationally in *Playboy*, the *Christian Science Monitor* and the *Washington Post*. Since December 1, 1979, he has also been La Varenne's United States Program Coordinator, organizing and accompanying chefs' tours in North America.

Allegro

Dinner for Six

Peperoni Arrosti
(Fresh-Roasted Peppers with an Aromatic Vinaigrette)

Fettuccine con Panna
(Homemade Noodles with Cream and Cheese)

Pesce Spada alla Griglia con Salsa Verde
(Grilled Swordfish with a Tart Green Sauce)

Zucchini Trifolati
(Sautéed Zucchini)

Zuccotto
(Pumpkin-Shaped Tuscan Cake Soaked in Liqueurs
and Served Semi-Frozen)

Wine:

With Fettuccine—Lugana (Salvalai) 1978
With Swordfish—Meursault Poruzots (Ropiteau) 1976

David and Lillian Coltin, Proprietors and Chefs

"It wasn't easy opening a Northern Italian restaurant in this area," recall Lillian and David Coltin, the youthful proprietors of Allegro in Waltham. Expecting the enormous servings awash in tomato sauce typical of most Anglo-Italian restaurants, the public was at first mystified by the delicacy and sophistication of Allegro's offerings. Some people, accustomed to filling up on a single dish, complained that the portions of Allegro's carefully balanced 6-course meals were too small. "That's simply not Northern Italian cooking," say the Coltins, who have gradually trained their clients to accord Allegro's fare the respect once reserved exclusively for French haute cuisine.

"People are amazed at the amount of effort we go through to cook things to order," remark the Coltins. The Coltins use a specially aged Asiago cheese for grating and insist on fresh Italian parsley for sauces, instead of the "curly green stuff." Meats are cooked on a grill, not under the broiler, for extra moistness and flavor.

"We've always wanted to open a restaurant," says David Coltin, whose employment prospects as a graduate student in English looked less than promising three years ago. The pair trained with Madeleine Kamman, before embarking on a gourmet tour of Northern Italy. It took them two years to find their Moody Street storefront and transform what was once a seedy neighborhood bar into a spacious, quietly elegant dining establishment. "Our food does the talking for us, so we've kept the décor and service as simple as possible," says David. "*Allegro* means 'joyful, pleasant, enjoyable' in Italian," adds Lillian, "and that's what restaurant dining should be."

For Lillian and David Coltin, the restaurant business remains a learning experience. "A person doesn't cook here long if I can't learn something from him," says David. "One of our cooks works miracles with pasta. Another lived extensively in Portugal and has the flavor of the Mediterranean at his fingertips. The notion that there is one single genius in the kitchen creating everything is false. Here at Allegro, our cuisine is a team effort."

458 MOODY STREET
WALTHAM

PEPERONI ARROSTI

Red peppers are at their best in October, when they are heavy and fleshy. The roasting brings out their sweetness and makes them easier to peel.

6 medium sweet peppers
Salt
Vinaigrette Sauce
1 tablespoon oregano
2 tablespoons capers, well rinsed
4 cloves garlic, peeled and bruised

1. Preheat the broiler for 15 minutes.
2. Select a nice mix of red, yellow and green peppers for a colorful presentation. Cut each pepper in half lengthwise and remove stems, seeds and core. Flatten peppers to expose as much skin surface as possible and arrange by color on baking sheets (the different types of peppers will cook at different rates).
3. Reduce broiler temperature if possible and place the peppers under the flame until the skin puffs and chars. Peel off as much skin as possible with your fingers, then trim off any remaining skin with a paring knife.
4. Choose a deep, flat dish in which the peppers can be presented at the table. Place a layer of peppers in the dish, alternating rows of red, green and yellow. Sprinkle lightly with salt. Spoon some **Vinaigrette Sauce** over the peppers and top with oregano, capers and garlic. Repeat this procedure with another layer of peppers and **Vinaigrette Sauce**. Marinate for at least 6 hours before serving.

Note: This dish can be prepared ahead of time, but remove the garlic cloves after 6 hours to avoid a bitter taste.

Vinaigrette Sauce

¼ cup red wine vinegar
½ teaspoon salt
1 anchovy filet
1 cup olive oil

1. Whirl the wine vinegar, salt and anchovy in a blender.
2. Gradually dribble in the olive oil and mix well.

The most important thing in all these recipes is being able to distinguish between mediocre ingredients and top quality ingredients. If you don't go to the trouble of finding good peppers or swordfish, the results just won't be the same.

FETTUCCINE CON PANNA

Our pasta, dried, tastes better than most I've sampled fresh. That's because we use only eggs, olive oil, flour and semolina. There's no water in the dough at all. We cook our pasta in individual saucepans at the restaurant, not in a single pot of boiling water which gets gummy and starchy during the course of the evening. We cook the sauce for the pasta in individual saucepans, too.

Pasta

2½ cups all-purpose flour (we use King Arthur)
½ cup semolina
Pinch of salt
4 large eggs, plus 1 extra yolk
1 tablespoon olive oil

1. Combine the dry ingredients in the bowl of a sturdy electric mixer. Stop the machine and make a depression in the center of the dry ingredients with your hand. Mix the wet ingredients in a separate bowl and pour into the center of the dry ingredients. Start the machine again and mix on the lowest speed. Transfer dough onto a floured surface and knead for 10 minutes with the heel of your palm.
2. Divide the pasta dough into 4 equal parts and keep covered with a clean dish cloth. Set your pasta machine to its widest setting. Pass each of the 4 balls of dough through the rollers 8 times, folding the dough in half each time.

3. Close the rollers to the next setting and feed the dough through without folding. Continue changing the roller setting until the dough is quite thin—about $1/32$".

4. Dry the sheets of dough on towels for about 20 minutes—they should cut cleanly into 10" sections. Feed the sheets of dough through the machine's fettuccine cutters and leave the noodles to dry on a towel until ready to use.

5. To cook the pasta, bring 4 gallons of water and 1 tablespoon of salt to a rolling boil. Add the fresh fettuccine and cook for 3 to 4 minutes. Do not overcook, as the pasta will continue cooking in the **Cream Sauce**. Drain the fettuccine and do not rinse.

Cream Sauce

1½ cups heavy cream
½ cup plus 2 tablespoons unsalted butter

Combine cream and butter in a 12" skillet and cook over medium heat for 5 minutes or until the mixture thickens slightly.

To finish:

Salt and freshly ground black pepper to taste
1¼ cups freshly grated Parmigiano Reggiano cheese

Add the cooked fettuccine, salt, pepper and grated cheese to the **Cream Sauce**. Stir over a medium-low heat until the cheese dissolves and thickens the cream. The noodles should be thoroughly coated. Serve in soup bowls with extra black pepper and grated cheese on the side.

Note: Semolina is a high protein durum wheat flour. Its high gluten content helps the noodles hold their shape. Semolina can be purchased in most Italian groceries and health food stores.

PESCE SPADA ALLA GRIGLIA CON SALSA VERDE

It is important that the fish be fresh, not previously frozen, and bought during the high season—summer and fall—when it is most flavorful. Sure you can buy swordfish year 'round in this country. The question is "do you want to?" Although the following recipe can be executed with a home broiler, nothing equals the flavor obtained from charcoal grilling.

1 cup olive oil
⅓ cup fresh lemon juice
Salt
6 swordfish steaks (approximately ½ pound per person)
Salsa Verde

1. Combine the olive oil, lemon juice and salt. Marinate the fish in the mixture for 30 minutes prior to grilling.
2. Ignite the charcoal, allowing the coals to turn white before placing the fish on the grill. Grill the swordfish steaks 3 to 5 minutes per side, depending on the thickness of the fish. The steaks are cooked when an inserted skewer comes out warm to the touch.
3. For serving, place a dab of **Salsa Verde** on each steak and pass the remaining sauce on the side.

Salsa Verde

¼ cup finely chopped Italian parsley
3 tablespoons capers, rinsed, drained and finely chopped
6 anchovy filets, finely chopped and mashed
1 teaspoon minced garlic
1 teaspoon Dijon-style mustard
1½ tablespoons fresh lemon juice
1 cup olive oil
Pinch of salt

1. Place the parsley, capers, anchovy filets and garlic in a small bowl. Whisk in the mustard and lemon juice.
2. Gradually beat in the olive oil, adding salt and additional lemon juice to taste if necessary.

ZUCCHINI TRIFOLATI

8 small, fresh, glossy zucchini
1 large onion, very thinly sliced
2 tablespoons unsalted butter
2 tablespoons corn oil
Salt

1. Soak the zucchini in cold water for 20 minutes to remove sand or grit. Dry and slice as thinly as possible.
2. Sauté the onion in butter and oil until golden. Add the zucchini and sprinkle lightly with salt. Stir the vegetables, shaking the pan over a medium heat for 2 minutes or until the zucchini becomes translucent.
3. Season to taste and serve at once.

What makes a good chef is the willingness to taste as you go along. I tell the kitchen help, "I want you to taste this dish until you feel like you never want to see it again." By the end of a busy evening, I feel as though someone has rubbed cotton batting across my palate. You still have a responsibility to the client to taste each dish before it goes out.

ZUCCOTTO

This recipe has been graciously provided by our friend Anna Tomasi Nathanson, a first-rate Italian cook and teacher from Florence, Italy.

Pan Di Spagna
Sponge Cake

6 eggs, separated
1 cup plus 2 tablespoons sugar
1 tablespoon vanilla
2 cups less 2 tablespoons sifted flour
2 tablespoons cornstarch

1. Butter and flour a square 9" cake pan.
2. Preheat the oven to 350°.
3. Beat yolks, 1 cup sugar and vanilla by hand or in a mixer until the mixture falls from the whisk in a thick ribbon.
4. In a separate bowl, beat the egg whites to soft peaks and sprinkle in the remaining two tablespoons of sugar. Continue beating until stiff.
5. Stir a quarter of the stiffly beaten egg whites into the yolk mixture to lighten it, then carefully fold in the remaining whites. Sift the flour and cornstarch over the egg mixture and gently fold in the flour.
6. Pour the batter into the pan and bake in preheated oven for 40 minutes or until an inserted skewer comes out clean. Turn the sponge cake onto a cake rack and cool completely.

Filling

2 cups heavy cream
¾ cup confectioners' sugar
2 ounces blanched almonds, toasted and chopped
3 ounces chocolate chips, chopped
¼ cup unsweetened cocoa

1. Whip the cream with the confectioners' sugar until very stiff.
2. Divide cream into 2 bowls and fold the chopped almonds into one.
   In the other bowl fold in the chocolate chips and cocoa.

To assemble:

¼ cup Cognac
¼ cup Cointreau
¼ cup maraschino liqueur

1. Combine the liqueurs in a shallow dish.
2. Cut the sponge cake into slices ³/₈" thick and soak the slices in the
   mixture of liqueurs for 10 minutes.
3. Choose a perfectly round 1½-quart bowl and line it with damp
   cheesecloth.
4. Line the bowl completely with cake slices, leaving no gaps through
   which the filling can escape.
5. Spoon the cream-almond mixture into the cake-lined bowl, followed
   by the cream-chocolate mixture. Place the remaining cake slices on
   top and cover with waxed paper.
6. Freeze for at least 3 hours, but remove from freezer ½ hour
   before serving. Invert onto a round platter and serve at once.

Café Budapest

Dinner for Six

Chilled Tart Cherry Soup à la Budapest

Chicken Paprikas

Marinated Cucumber Salad

Fresh Raspberries with Grand Marnier Sauce

Wine:

With Cherry Soup—Badacsony Szürkebarat
With Chicken Paprikas—Tokaji Szamorodni
With Dessert—Tokaji Aszu 5 Puttonyos

Edith Ban, Proprietor

Every evening at half past eight, a woman with regal bearing in a long white evening gown sweeps through the Café Budapest. As she passes, the maître d' snaps to attention, the waiters bustle more briskly and even the clients pause between forkfuls, struck by an inexplicable but undeniable feeling of awe. The woman is Edith Ban, proud owner of the Café Budapest. There is no doubt in anyone's mind who is boss.

To look at Mrs. Ban today, one would never guess that she came to the United States a refugee from the 1956 Hungarian Revolution and that during her first three months in Massachusetts she worked as a maid on Cape Cod. Unhappy working for others, she soon opened a small espresso bar next to Beth Israel Hospital in Brookline. By 1965, she had amassed the resources and cooking experience necessary to open a restaurant in the basement of the Lenox Hotel downtown. The Café Budapest started with four employees; today it has a staff of seventy. It is not uncommon for the Café Budapest to serve 500 dinners on a busy Saturday night.

"I still work in the kitchen," says the chic Mrs. Ban who prepares the restaurant's soups and sauces. She developed all the recipes used at the Café Budapest and the chefs are expected to follow these recipes to the letter. "The chefs may change, the food does not change at the Café Budapest," she insists. "We have no steam table or fryolator in the kitchen, so all of our central European fare is prepared to order."

The majesty and romance of the Austro-Hungarian empire still flourish at the Café Budapest. Guests are seated in three stately dining areas: the oak-paneled Hungarian Room, the elegant Pink Room and a charming, gingerbread-house-like Weinstube. In the Budapest bar, with its Empire fauteuils and flocked wallpaper, guests can sip heady Viennese coffee or golden Hungarian dessert wine and listen to the gypsy musicians who often fill the room with their haunting tunes.

90 EXETER STREET
BOSTON

CHILLED TART CHERRY SOUP A LA BUDAPEST

This recipe calls for tart or sour cherries. You just won't get the same results if you use Bing cherries or substitute light cream for medium cream.

2 (16-ounce) cans of pitted tart cherries, 1 can drained, 1 can with
    liquid reserved
1 large cinnamon stick
10 whole cloves
10 whole allspice berries
1 thin slice lemon
½ cup sugar
Pinch of salt
1½ teaspoons flour
1 cup medium cream
¾ cup dry red Burgundy
½ cup heavy cream

1. Combine the cherries, cherry juice, spices, lemon, sugar and salt
   in a saucepan and bring to a boil for 2 minutes.
2. Mix the flour with a few tablespoons medium cream to make a thick
   paste. Stir this paste into the remaining medium cream.
3. Add the cream and wine to the cherry mixture and boil for 1 minute.
   Remove the soup from the heat and let cool, then refrigerate.
4. To serve, ladle into soup bowls. Beat the heavy cream to stiff peaks
   and place a spoonful of cream on each serving.

Note: This soup will keep in the refrigerator for up to 2 weeks.

There is nothing difficult about these recipes. If you bring a little love to your cooking, you can prepare anything.

CHICKEN PAPRIKAS

We only use butter and chicken fat in our cooking at the Café Budapest.

Paprika has been used in Hungary since the fifteenth century. We have the best paprika in the world because our climate is so well suited to its cultivation. People think Hungarian paprika is spicy. It is tasty and flavorful, but not spicy.

This recipe feeds eight to ten.

2 tomatoes, peeled, seeded and coarsely chopped
1 cup chicken fat
2 medium onions, finely chopped
2 cloves garlic, crushed
2 green peppers, cored, seeded and thinly sliced
2 (1½-pound) chickens, each cut into 8 pieces (2 thighs, 2 drumsticks,
    2 breast-wing pieces, 2 breast pieces)
2 tablespoons Hungarian paprika
½ teaspoon hot Italian crushed pepper
2 cups chicken stock or 4 bouillon cubes plus 2
    cups water (approximately)
3 tablespoons flour
1 pint sour cream
1 cup medium cream
Salt and pepper
Nockerl

1. To peel the tomatoes, score an "x" on the bottoms, immerse in boiling water for 10 seconds, rinse under cold water and slip off skins. Set aside.
2. Melt the chicken fat in a heavy pan and sauté onions over high heat until transparent and straw colored. Lower heat and add the garlic, green peppers and tomatoes. Sauté until peppers are soft and golden. Add the chicken pieces and lightly sauté—the meat should not be allowed color.
3. Add the paprika, crushed red pepper and enough chicken stock to cover. Gently simmer over a low heat for approximately 20 minutes or until the chicken is cooked. (The juices will run clear when the meat is pricked with a fork.) Remove chicken from sauce and keep warm.
4. Whisk the flour into the sour cream and medium cream to make a cold roux. Whisk this roux into the sauce, bring the sauce to a boil and boil for 1 minute or until the sauce thickens.

5. Correct the seasoning. Strain the sauce onto the chicken and serve with **Nockerl**.

Nockerl

6 whole eggs
¼ cup butter, melted and cooled
1 teaspoon salt
2 to 2½ cups flour
Butter

1. Beat the eggs with the melted butter and salt.
2. Mix in the flour by hand to obtain a thick, stiff dough. Knead lightly and pat into a flat oblong.
3. Bring a large pot of salted water to a boil. Lay the dough on a small cutting board and cut off ⅛" strips of dough with the edge of a spatula directly into the boiling water.
4. Cook for 1 minute, then remove with a slotted spoon and drain. Toss with butter for serving.

Hungary is one of the oldest wine-producing countries in the world. The Romans imported Hungarian wine to Italy. Louis XIV preferred Hungarian Tokaji with fish. We serve only Hungarian wines at the Café Budapest and we have one of the most extensive selections in the country.

MARINATED CUCUMBER SALAD

I had never seen the inside of a restaurant kitchen before I opened the Budapest. If I had, I would surely have chosen another profession!

3 large cucumbers, peeled and thinly sliced
1 small onion, thinly sliced
1 green pepper, cored, seeded and thinly sliced
½ cup sour cream

For the marinade:

1 cup white vinegar
½ cup sugar
2 cloves garlic, peeled and bruised
Salt and freshly ground black pepper

Combine the ingredients for the marinade and marinate the cucumbers for as long or as little as you like. (You can serve them immediately or marinate them for up to 2 weeks.) Serve cucumbers with onion and green pepper on chilled salad plates, with a spoonful of sour cream on top.

There is nothing so perfect that it cannot be improved.

In Hungary we have a problem of what to eat. In America they have a problem of what not to eat!

FRESH RASPBERRIES WITH GRAND MARNIER SAUCE

3 cups fresh raspberries
Dry red wine
5 egg yolks
½ cup plus 2 tablespoons sugar
½ cup Grand Marnier
1 cup heavy cream

1. Wash the raspberries in red wine, drain and set aside.
2. Beat the yolks with ½ cup sugar in a stainless steel bowl over a pot of hot water. Beat for 10 minutes or until the yolk mixture falls from the whisk in a thick ribbon. Remove from heat and stir in half the Grand Marnier. Let the sauce come to room temperature, then refrigerate until completely chilled.
3. Beat the cream with the remaining sugar to semi-stiff peaks. Gently fold the cream into the chilled yolk mixture with the remaining Grand Marnier.
4. Serve the raspberries in chilled champagne glasses, with the sauce spooned over the top.

When we put a dish on the menu, we always serve it at the price marked. If the cost of the ingredients has skyrocketed, that's too bad for us.

The Café Plaza

Dinner for Four

Oysters Kirkpatrick

Watercress Salad with Lemon-Walnut Dressing

Côtes de Boeuf Sauce Roquefort
(Prime Rib Steaks with Roquefort Sauce)

Freddy's Roast Potatoes

Strawberries Flambée

Wine:

With Oysters—Chardonnay (Freemark Abbey) 1976
With Meat—Gevrey-Chambertin Domaine Poulette
(Villamont) 1972

Lydia Shire, Chef

"A hotel isn't supposed to have such good food," a client once joked with the chef of the Café Plaza. "We run our restaurant as a restaurant, not a convenience eatery for hotel guests," was the quick, but convivial reply. The hotel is that grande dame of Boston hostelry, the Copley Plaza. The chef is Cordon Bleu-trained Lydia Shire, who came to Copley's Café Plaza three years ago and has garnered Best of Boston awards every year of her tenure.

The soft-spoken Lydia Shire is something of an anomaly at the Copley Plaza Hotel, where she commands an all-male kitchen. Until the mid-fifties, the Café Plaza functioned as a men's bar and no woman, chef or otherwise, dared to cross its leaded-glass portals.

Built in 1912 as the sister hotel to New York's renowned Park Plaza Hotel, the Copley still retains the splendor of the turn of the century. Waterford crystal chandeliers cast a soft glow on the handsome oak *boiserie* of the Café Plaza dining room. Tuxedoed maître d's glide discreetly beneath one of Boston's most ornate stucco ceilings. With such luxurious appointments, one can easily see why the Café Plaza was named by United Airline's *Mainliner* magazine as one of the ten most romantic restaurants in the United States.

"There's nothing I serve that I don't taste before it goes to the dining room," says Lydia Shire. The menu, which Shire describes as two-thirds classical French and one-third experimental, changes weekly. The Café Plaza wine list—stocked with the finest vintages of the last century—has received national attention. "We never advertise our cuisine, though," says Shire. "Our reputation speaks loudly enough for itself."

COPLEY PLAZA
BOSTON

OYSTERS KIRKPATRICK

I have always liked the name of this dish. It's very Irish and very Boston.

The oysters you buy should be dirty. When oysters come out of the water, they live off the silt and grit on the shell. Clean oysters may look pretty, but they're actually starving to death.

16 large fresh oysters in the shell
Marinara Sauce
1 small green pepper, cored, seeded and finely diced
1 cup grated sharp Cheddar cheese, like Coon cheese
2 strips bacon, cut into 16 (1") squares

1. Preheat oven to 450°.
2. Scrub the oysters thoroughly and open them not more than 20 minutes before you plan to serve them.
3. Set oysters on the half shell on a baking sheet and spoon 1 teaspoon **Marinara Sauce** over each oyster. Place 1 teaspoon diced green peppers on top of the sauce. Sprinkle the oysters with cheese and top with a square of bacon.
4. Just prior to serving, bake in preheated oven for 5 to 7 minutes or until the bacon starts to crisp around the edges. Serve immediately.

Marinara Sauce

3 cloves garlic, minced
¼ cup olive oil
1 small can Italian plum tomatoes, drained and chopped
Pinch of oregano
¼ cup fresh chopped parsley
Salt and freshly ground black pepper to taste

Sauté the garlic in olive oil, but do not let brown. Add the tomatoes, oregano, parsley, salt and pepper and simmer for 10 minutes. Let the sauce cool before using in the recipe above.

Use a recipe as a guideline, not a computer program. When I look at a recipe, I never read the amounts. I consider the ingredient combinations, then I let my imagination run free.

WATERCRESS SALAD WITH LEMON-WALNUT DRESSING

When choosing watercress, look for a bright emerald green color. Avoid bunches with yellow spots. . . . I hate when people cut the ends off of lemon wedges. I hate when people snap off the pretty ends of string beans. I like my food to look the way it does in nature.

2 bunches watercress
½ clove garlic
Salt and pepper
Juice of 1 to 2 lemons
Pinch of oregano
½ cup walnut oil
Lemon wedges

1. Wash the watercress, shake to remove excess water and twist off the coarse stems. Place in a plastic bag in the refrigerator for 1 hour to crisp.
2. Mash the garlic with the salt. Combine with lemon juice, oregano and pepper in a salad bowl.
3. Whisk in the walnut oil little by little to obtain an emulsified dressing. Correct the seasoning, adding additional lemon juice if necessary.
4. Gently toss the watercress with the dressing. Serve on chilled salad plates with lemon wedges for garnish.

My advice to nonprofessionals is to not be afraid to undercook foods. Beef tastes best rare; fish is more delicate slightly undercooked; vegetables taste better left slightly al dente. The worst thing you can do to most food is to overcook it.

COTES DE BOEUF SAUCE ROQUEFORT

You have to use genuine French Roquefort cheese for this dish. Blue cheese simply does not have the right flavor. . . . The clue to good meat is the color. Beef which is bright red is too young. Look for a darker blood-brown color, which indicates that the beef has been well aged. As soon as you get meat home from the market, remove the plastic wrapping; beef which sits in the package gets all wet and soggy. You want the meat to roast when you cook it, not steam.

Salt and freshly ground black pepper
2 prime double-rib steaks (3" thick) with the bone left in and the end
    of the rib "Frenched," or scraped clean
Vegetable oil

1. Preheat oven to 400°.
2. Salt and pepper the steaks heavily and brown one side darkly in hot oil in a large skillet. Pour off fat, invert steaks and roast meat in the frying pan for about 20 minutes. (Rare beef will feel slightly springy when pressed with a finger.)
3. Remove the beef from the oven and let rest for 10 minutes.
4. To serve, carve each steak toward the bone into ¼" slices. Arrange these slices on hot dinner plates. Serve with **Sauce Roquefort** on the side.

Sauce Roquefort

4 ounces genuine French Roquefort cheese
½ cup unsalted butter
1 bottle dry white wine
¾ cup heavy cream
Salt and freshly ground black pepper, if necessary

1. Mash the Roquefort cheese with the butter and beat with a wooden spoon or whisk until the mixture is smooth and creamy.
2. Pour the wine into a saucepan and boil until only ⅓ cup remains. Add the cream and reduce again by boiling until only ⅓ cup liquid remains.
3. Reduce heat to low and whisk in the cheese-butter mixture, 2 tablespoons at a time. At no point should the sauce boil.
4. Strain sauce and taste for seasoning—you will probably not need salt because the cheese is very salty. The sauce can be prepared ahead of time and kept at a blood-warm temperature over hot water.

FREDDY'S ROAST POTATOES

This is the greatest roast potato dish in the world. The recipe comes from my boyfriend Freddy King, who is a captain in one of our other restaurants, Copley's. . . . The skin of the garlic must be completely intact, or the garlic will burn and go bitter. Do not use cloves with skins which are split or cracked. The garlic can be discarded or eaten— the whole roast cloves look very pretty with the potatoes.

4 Idaho or large Red Bliss potatoes, peeled and quartered
Salt and freshly ground black pepper
10 cloves unpeeled garlic
½ cup unsalted butter

1. Preheat oven to 400°.
2. Boil the potatoes in salted water for exactly 10 minutes, then drain. This can be done up to 24 hours ahead of time.
3. Place potatoes in a roasting pan just large enough to accommodate them without crowding. Sprinkle liberally with salt and pepper. Add the unpeeled garlic cloves and dot the potatoes with butter.
4. Roast in preheated oven for 30 minutes or until well browned, turning the potatoes once or twice to assure even roasting. Serve with or without garlic according to taste.

Correct seasoning is the cook's first duty. The client should never need to pick up a salt or pepper shaker. When I'm served a dish in a restaurant, I assume the chef has seasoned the food as he meant for me to taste it. If there's not enough salt or pepper, that's too bad.

STRAWBERRIES FLAMBEE

I never thought I would like Strawberries Flambée. I don't believe in cooking fruits like berries. But one evening, after a particularly grueling service, our maître d' Heinz Bunger prepared this dish for me and it was wonderful!

2 pints strawberries, washed, hulled and halved
3 tablespoons sugar
Juice of ½ lemon
2 ounces strawberry-flavored brandy
2 tablespoons butter
Sprinkle of cinnamon
2 ounces Cognac

1. Place strawberries in a shallow bowl with 2 tablespoons sugar, the lemon juice and strawberry-flavored brandy and let marinate for 10 minutes, turning once.
2. Heat a sauté pan over a chafing dish and add the remaining sugar and butter, cooking until the mixture caramelizes. Quickly add the strawberries and marinade and sprinkle with cinnamon.
3. Pour the Cognac over the fruit and ignite. Remove the berries after 30 seconds—they should be barely warmed, not cooked—and finish flambéing the sauce. Serve the strawberries plain, on ice cream or with whipped cream, spooning the sauce on top. Serve at once.

Casa Romero

Dinner for Four

Sangrita
(Spicy Apéritif Served with Tequila)

Caldo de Mejillones
(Steamed Mussels in Herbed Wine Broth)

Ensalada de Guacamole
(Traditional Avocado Dip)

Puerco Adobado
(Pork Tenderloin Marinated with Oranges
and Smoked Peppers)

Arroz à la Mexicana
(Mexican Rice)

Flan al Coñac
(Traditional Custard with Cognac)

Beer:

Light—Superior or Carta Blanca
Dark—Dos Equis

Leo Romero, Proprietor

"I started in the food business because there were no decent Mexican restaurants in New England," says Back Bay restaurateur Leo Romero. Armed with an innate ability to cook and the unshakable conviction that authentic Mexican fare could rival any cuisine in the world, Leo opened the Casa Romero on the ground floor of a Gloucester Street townhouse in 1972. "The menu was already printed and I had no idea how we were going to manage some of the dishes in a restaurant kitchen," he says, recalling the early days with a smile. Manage he did, though, and before long the Casa Romero was ranked the top Mexican restaurant outside of Mexico by *Gourmet Magazine* and one of the ten best restaurants in the United States by the German guide book *Bessers*.

"Mexico has always had an exquisite cuisine," says Romero. "In Aztec times, fresh fish reached Mexico City more quickly by runner than it does by truck or locomotive today. When the Emperor Montezuma craved ice cream, he dispatched his cooks to fetch snow from the nearby mountains. Many modern Mexican specialties were invented during the Baroque period, when Mexico had one of the wealthiest aristocracies in the world."

The Mexican cuisine of the Casa Romero has little in common with the tacos and enchiladas of fast food chains, the mere thought of which makes Romero bristle. "Some of our sauces take three days to prepare, using dozens of ingredients, which must be specially and individually processed beforehand."

When it comes to Mexican cooking, Romero should know what he's talking about. The son of a Spanish-American diplomat and a Franco-Mexican mother, he grew up in Mexico, inhabiting all of the major provinces. "I have never set foot in a cooking school and I've trained some of the finest chefs in Boston," he says with pride. "I am a cook by avocation, by instinct, by love."

"When you open the door of the Casa Romero, you walk out of Back Bay and into Mexico," observes Romero. Colorful tile tables, straight-backed leather chairs, ornate wrought iron and Mexican handicrafts create the atmosphere of a Spanish colonial mansion. You also enter Leo Romero's home. "I consider the dining room downstairs an extension of my own dinner table," says Romero, who lives on the top two floors of the building. "I receive my clients not so much as customers, but as guests."

30 GLOUCESTER STREET
BOSTON

SANGRITA

Sangrita traditionally accompanies tequila and both are drunk before the meal, never at the table. In Mexico everyone has an individual version of Sangrita; the recipe below is mine.

1 cup unsweetened grapefruit juice
1 cup tomato juice
1 tablespoon juice from canned or bottled jalapeño peppers
2 tablespoons grenadine

Combine ingredients and serve in cordial glasses.

Mexican cooking is probably the most misunderstood cuisine in the world. If you study the history of Mexico, if you understand the geography and the people, it will become clear to you that the haute cuisine of Mexico is much more embellished, much more elaborate, much more lavish than the cuisines of France or the Austro-Hungarian Empire.

CALDO DE MEJILLONES

We use aquacultured mussels, which contain virtually no sand or grit.

2 pounds mussels
1 medium onion, very finely chopped
½ cup unsalted butter
1 cup finely chopped parsley
Salt and freshly ground black pepper to taste
1 cup dry white wine

1. Wash the mussels in several changes of cold water, thoroughly scrubbing the shells. Remove threads and discard any mussels with cracked shells or which fail to close when tapped.
2. Sauté the onion in butter in a large saucepan until transparent. Add the parsley and a little salt and pepper. Pour in the wine and boil to reduce the mixture by half.
3. Place the mussels in the pan, cover, reduce heat and steam for 5 minutes or until the shells open. Serve the mussels and broth in deep bowls with an extra bowl on the side to hold the empty shells.

I don't approve of making a sacrament of fine food. Food should be enjoyed as a gustatory and biological necessity.

ENSALADA DE GUACAMOLE

The guacamole below is made with spicy Casera Sauce. Be sure to use very ripe California avocados. Florida does not grow avocados—it grows alligator pears and there is a difference. . . . There is no substitute for cilantro, the pungent leaves of the coriander plant. Cilantro can be found in most Hispanic, Chinese and natural food markets—it often goes by the name of Chinese parsley.

3 ripe avocados
1 cup **Casera Sauce**
4 large lettuce leaves
Fried tortilla chips

1. Peel the avocados and remove the seeds. Mash the flesh in a non-metallic bowl and gradually work in the **Casera Sauce**.
2. Mound the guacamole on lettuce leaves on 4 serving plates and serve with tortilla chips.

Casera Sauce

This makes two cups sauce. Use the remaining cup for the rice.

4 large ripe tomatoes
½ cup finely chopped onion
1 jalapeño pepper, finely chopped (the canned peppers are actually a
    little tastier than the fresh ones, because they are marinated
    in vinegar)
¼ cup finely chopped cilantro
1 tablespoon olive oil
½ teaspoon crumbled oregano
Salt and freshly ground black pepper

1. Slice off the stem end of the tomato and grate tomato into a shallow bowl. (Grating peels the tomato at the same time.)
2. Add the remaining ingredients and mix.

The best cooks in Mexico are illiterate for the most part. They are the maids, the peasant women, who have been cooking for generations and generations—almost forever.

PUERCO ADOBADO

In Mexico, the pork would be marinated in the juice of the naranja agria, *an orange with an intensely tart flavor. One can achieve the same effect in this country with canned orange juice concentrate. There is no substitute for the chipotle pepper, however, with its unique smoky flavor. It's available canned in many good gourmet shops.*

¼ cup oil
Juice of 1 lemon
½ cup orange juice concentrate
Grated rind of 1 orange
1 clove garlic, peeled
2 chipotle peppers
1 teaspoon salt
2 pounds pork tenderloin
1 orange, thinly sliced

1. To prepare the marinade, purée all the ingredients except the pork and orange slices in a blender.
2. Place pork in a shallow dish and spread all surfaces with the orange mixture. Marinate the pork in the refrigerator for at least 3 hours, preferably overnight.
3. One hour before cooking, remove the pork from the refrigerator. Preheat the broiler.
4. Transfer pork to a roasting pan and broil for 10 minutes. Turn the meat and broil for 5 more minutes or until the pork is thoroughly cooked. (The marinade "cooks" the meat, so the overall cooking time will be reduced.) Do not overcook or the meat will be dry.
5. Garnish pork with orange slices for serving.

Although lard is the preferred fat of Mexico, we don't use it much any more, because it's not particularly healthy. Nutrition and health play an important part in what we eat. So we've replaced the lard in most dishes with a good polyunsaturated vegetable oil.

ARROZ A LA MEXICANA

Use real long-grain rice, not Minute Rice or Uncle Ben's. In general, the cheaper the rice, the better it is.

It is essential that the rice be tightly covered during cooking, so that it steams, rather than boils.

2 cups unpolished long-grain rice
½ cup chicken fat or vegetable oil
½ cup **Casera Sauce** (remainder from guacamole)
4 cups homemade chicken stock
Salt and freshly ground black pepper

1. Wash and rinse the rice in several changes of water to remove excess starch. Spread on a cookie sheet to dry.
2. Sauté the rice in fat in a large cast-iron frying pan until the grains are uniformly light brown.
3. Reduce heat to the lowest flame and stir in the remaining ingredients. Press a sheet of tin foil over the rice and cover with a heavy lid.
4. Cook over a low heat for 20 minutes. Do not uncover the pan or stir. Make sure the pan is correctly centered over the flame. When the rice is cooked, fluff with a fork and correct the seasoning before serving.

FLAN AL COÑAC

Unlike the Spanish version of this dessert favorite, the Mexican flan is richly flavored with spices and brandy. It unmolds more easily if served the following day.

3 cups milk
4 eggs
1¾ cups sugar
⅔ teaspoon vanilla extract
⅓ teaspoon nutmeg
⅓ teaspoon cinnamon
⅓ teaspoon ground allspice
3 tablespoons Cognac
Pinch of salt

1. Preheat oven to 350°.
2. Scald the milk, but do not boil. Set aside to cool.
3. Beat the eggs well with ¼ cup sugar, vanilla, nutmeg, cinnamon, allspice, Cognac and salt. Whisk in the cooled milk.
4. Place remaining sugar with water to cover in a heavy, non-tin-lined saucepan. Cook over a high heat without stirring until the mixture attains a rich, golden caramel color.
5. Remove from heat and distribute the caramel evenly among 4 (6-ounce) ramekins. Swirl the cups to coat the sides and bottom of each dish. (Work carefully—molten caramel is extremely hot.)
6. Once the caramel has cooled, ladle the custard mixture into the cups and place cups in a shallow roasting pan with 1" of boiling water. Bake in preheated oven for 1 hour or until an inserted skewer comes out clean. Cool completely before serving. To unmold, invert the ramekins over deep dishes and shake until the flan slips free.

cybele

ON THE WATERFRONT

Dinner for Four

Seafood Fettuccine

Chicken Fiorentina

Butter-Glazed Broccoli

Cybele's Salad

Tartelettes aux Pommes Chaudes Cazalis

Wine:

*With Fettuccine and Chicken—Orvieto Classico
(Le Veletti Estate) 1976
With Tartelettes—Holle Johannisberg Riesling Spätlese
(Weingut Hof Sonneck)*

*Rebecca Caras, Proprietor
Sara Moulton, Chef*

Five years ago, Rebecca Caras got her start in the food business cooking for friends out of her home. Today she rules a culinary empire which includes a catering enterprise, two gourmet carry-out shops and a pair of highly praised restaurants. A few years ago the Rouse Company, developers of Faneuil Hall, asked Rebecca to open a small tearoom in the basement of the then-unrenovated South Market. Within months the tearoom became a nationally acclaimed restaurant and it has recently moved to a more spacious and luxurious setting on the waterfront. "Cybele was the mythological daughter of Earth and Sky and to the ancient Greeks she symbolized plentitude and pleasure," says Caras. "We hope Cybele's holds the same meaning for our guests."

Caras describes Cybele's fare as "eclectic seasonal," uniting classical French cooking techniques with the bold flavors of the Mediterranean and the health consciousness of contemporary America. "We try to serve honest food, food which tastes similar to what a good cook would prepare at home," she says. Caras believes that the food and the people should be the main visual elements of any dining area. The exposed brick walls and ceiling beams, the stunning shades of grey, mauve and lavender of the three dining rooms provide a perfect foil for enjoying one's food and one's dinner companions at the new Cybele's.

"I have always been impassioned by food," says Caras. "It was how we expressed ourselves when we were growing up. My mother was a superb cook, who could take ingredients on any level and assemble them in a way which made sense. It's not an easy life," concedes Caras, who works seven days a week. "You have to commit yourself to a profession which involves a lot of compromise in the rest of your life. When you consider the hours, the working conditions, the heat, you understand why so many cooks are temperamental."

Cybele's chef, Sara Moulton, is just the opposite of the mercurial cook. The accomplished, affable young woman graduated second in her class of 450 at the Culinary Institute of America and served as associate chef of Julia Child's TV team before becoming Cybele's chef a year ago. For Sara, cooking is more than a job or an occupation. "I can be having a horrible day when everything seems to go wrong, but if I make a nice special and everyone in the dining room likes it, I'm in Seventh Heaven!"

240 COMMERCIAL STREET
BOSTON

SEAFOOD FETTUCCINE

The secret of cooking pasta is to watch it like crazy. We use Menucci pasta, which is the best dried pasta you can buy. We get the water really boiling, with a little oil to keep the noodles from sticking to one another. You have to stir continually while the pasta is cooking.

½ pound mussels
½ pound scallops
16 large shrimp
½ pound fish filet (use a white fish like sole, scrod or haddock)
2 cups dry vermouth
1 tablespoon finely chopped shallots
2 tablespoons unsalted butter
5 scallions, finely chopped
1 clove garlic, mashed
4 cups heavy cream
1 pound good dried fettuccine
1 cup freshly grated Parmesan cheese
¼ cup finely chopped fresh parsley
Salt and freshly ground black pepper to taste

continued

1. Thoroughly scrub the mussels and remove strings. Pull off the small, half-moon-shaped muscle from the scallops and cut scallops into uniform pieces. Peel and devein shrimp. Cut the fish into ½" x 2" slivers.
2. Bring the vermouth to a boil with the shallots. Add mussels, cover tightly and steam for 3 to 4 minutes or until the shells open. Remove mussels and strain broth through a cheesecloth or clean dish towel into a large saucepan.
3. Reheat the broth and gently poach the scallops (they should be barely cooked). Remove scallops with a slotted spoon and poach the shrimp until they begin to turn pink. Remove shrimp and poach the fish. (Each item will take 1 to 2 minutes to poach.)
4. Melt the butter in a large sauté pan and sauté the scallions and garlic until soft and translucent. Add the fish-poaching liquid and cream. Increase heat and boil the sauce until reduced by half.
5. Bring 6 quarts lightly salted water to a boil (a splash of oil helps prevent the fettuccine from sticking) and cook the fettuccine al dente—about 8 minutes. Drain, but do not rinse.
6. To finish, add the pasta to the reduced sauce and simmer for 1 minute. Stir in the seafood, cheese, parsley, salt and pepper. Simmer the mixture gently to warm the seafood.
7. Serve in bowls with a twist of freshly ground black pepper on top. Extra cheese should accompany the dish on the side.

To be a good chef, you have to be able to taste and to imagine taste. You have to be able to work with people, being both firm and supportive.

CHICKEN FIORENTINA

The hardest thing about this dish is the sauce. You want to end up with an emulsion of olive oil, lemon juice and vermouth—a lovely, silky, translucent sauce, like a butter sauce—it's very tricky.

4 plump artichokes
1 cup olive oil (approximately)
Juice of 3 lemons
Pinch of thyme
Salt and freshly ground black pepper
½ cup flour
4 boned chicken breasts, trimmed, cut in half lengthwise, then in
    quarters against the grain
1 cup vermouth
¼ cup finely chopped fresh parsley

1. Cut the tops and stems off the artichokes. Remove the tough outer leaves and quarter. Use a spoon or paring knife to remove the fibrous "choke" from the center of each artichoke quarter.
2. Place artichokes in a shallow pan with ½" olive oil, the juice of 2 lemons, a pinch of thyme, salt and pepper. Cover the pan and cook over low heat for 10 to 15 minutes or until the artichokes are tender. Drain and set aside.
3. Lightly flour the chicken and gently sauté for 3 to 4 minutes in the artichoke oil without browning. Do not cook too long—if anything, the chicken should remain a little undercooked. Remove chicken from pan and set aside.
4. Pour off all but 2 tablespoons oil from the pan. Add the vermouth, remaining lemon juice, another pinch of thyme, salt and pepper to the oil. Boil the sauce for 2 minutes. Return the chicken and artichokes to the pan to warm in the sauce. Stir in the parsley and serve at once.

BUTTER-GLAZED BROCCOLI

You should always use unsalted butter. It's of a much higher quality.
It's always fresher, because you can't disguise the rancidity with salt.
Besides, you want to add the salt to suit your own taste.

1 large bunch broccoli (about 2 pounds), trimmed of tough stems and
    cut into florets
1 cup water
¼ cup unsalted butter
Salt and freshly ground black pepper
1 small red onion, thinly sliced

1. Place broccoli, water, butter, salt and pepper in a saucepan and cook
   over high heat for 15 to 20 minutes or until most of the water
   evaporates and the broccoli is tender.
2. When the broccoli is almost done, add the red onion slices.

CYBELE'S SALAD

Cybele's Salad consists of lettuce leaves assembled to form a rosette. The R-A-C of RAC Dressing are Rebecca A. Caras's initials.

1 large or 2 small heads Boston lettuce
8 cherry tomatoes, cut in half
¼ cup chopped scallions
1 cup **RAC Dressing**

1. Wash and dry the lettuce, leaving the leaves whole.
2. Make 4 lettuce rosettes in the palm of your hand by laying successively smaller lettuce leaves on top of one another at right angles. If the lettuce has dark outside leaves, it's nice to alternate colors.
3. Garnish each lettuce rosette with cherry tomatoes and scallions. Spoon the **RAC Dressing** on top.

RAC Dressing

This makes one cup.

1 egg
2 tablespoons red wine vinegar
2½ tablespoons light cream
½ teaspoon lemon juice
½ teaspoon Dijon-style mustard
½ teaspoon sugar
1 clove garlic, minced
2 tablespoons olive oil
Scant half-cup vegetable oil
Salt and pepper to taste

1. Combine egg, vinegar, cream, lemon juice, mustard, sugar and garlic in a blender and mix.
2. Set the blender on low speed and gradually dribble in the oils. Season with salt and pepper before serving.

I don't like using food to intimidate people. You have to understand it, respect it, but you mustn't be afraid of it. Food is not a temple or a sacred involvement. Food is fun, it's humorous, it's an endless source of adventure.

TARTELETTES AUX POMMES CHAUDES CAZALIS

These hot apple tartlets were the house dessert at the Henri IV, a two-star restaurant in Chartres where Cybele's chef Sara Moulton apprenticed over the summer. The owner of the restaurant, Maurice Cazalis, is a maître cuisinier of France.

Pâte Sucrée
Sweet Pie Dough

2 cups flour
½ cup unsalted butter, cold, but softened by pounding
½ cup plus 2 tablespoons sugar
1 egg
Pinch of salt

1. Sift flour onto a counter top and make a well in the center. Break the butter into small pieces and place in the well along with the sugar, egg and salt.
2. Mix the ingredients in the center with your fingertips, gradually incorporating the flour to form largish crumbs. Knead these into a compact mass with the heel of your palm. Chill the dough for at least 20 minutes.
3. Preheat the oven to 400°.
4. Roll the dough on a lightly floured surface to a thickness of ⅛". Line 4 (6") tartlet pans with dough, pricking the bottoms with a fork to prevent the crusts from rising. Press a sheet of tin foil into each crust and fill the mold with dried beans or rice.
5. Refrigerate the tartlets for 10 minutes, then bake in preheated oven for 10 minutes. Remove the beans and tin foil and continue baking crusts 5 to 10 more minutes or until completely cooked, but not browned. Carefully remove crusts from tartlet pans and leave to cool on a cake rack.

Compôte Aux Pommes
Fresh Apple Sauce

2 apples (Rome or McIntosh will do fine), peeled, cored and cut
  into chunks
2 tablespoons sugar
1 tablespoon water
Juice of ½ lemon, plus a little grated rind
1 teaspoon vanilla

Combine the ingredients in a small saucepan and cook over a medium
heat until the apples dissolve, forming a thick purée. Remove from
heat and cool.

To finish:

4 firm apples (like Grannie Smiths or Golden Delicious), peeled
  and cored
½ cup sugar
Confectioners' sugar for sprinkling
1 cup softly whipped cream
1 cup sour cream

1. Preheat oven to 400°.
2. Prepare the remaining apples for baking. Using a sharp knife, make
   a series of parallel, vertical slashes ¼" apart. Turn the apple 90° and
   score in a similar fashion to achieve a crosshatch effect. Do not cut all
   the way through the apples—you want each piece of fruit to remain
   in 1 piece.
3. Sprinkle the 4 apples with sugar and bake in preheated oven for 20
   minutes or until the apples are browned and soft. The tartlets may
   be prepared ahead of time to this stage.
4. To assemble the tartlets, divide the compote evenly among the 4
   tartlet shells. Using a spatula, carefully place the baked apples in the
   center. Just before serving, warm in the oven and sprinkle with
   confectioners' sugar.
5. Combine the whipped cream and sour cream to make an American
   approximation of crème fraîche. Serve on the side.

*When you score the apples the first time, there is a very good chance
they'll fall apart. If this happens, you can piece them together with
toothpicks.*

PARKER'S

Dinner for Four

Parker House Rolls

Warm Marinated Mussels

Médaillons de Veau Cressonnière
(Veal Medallions with Watercress Sauce)

Hearts of Palm Vinaigrette

Strawberries Romanoff

Wine:

With Mussels—Pouilly-Fumé (St. Laurent) 1977
With Veal—Meursault (Jaboulet Vercherre)
With Dessert—Dom Pérignon (Moët et Chandon) 1971

Joseph Ribas, Chef

In 1825 a young man set out from Paris, Maine, with the clothes on his back and less than a dollar in his pocket to find his fortune in Boston. Thirty years later, he built a gleaming marble edifice on the corner of Tremont and School Streets, destined to become the premier hotel in New England. Harvey Parker rose from stable boy to restaurateur to millionaire. His hotel and dining establishment, the Parker House, has remained synonymous with high class and hospitality for 126 years.

"To dine here is to live," pronounced one enthusiast when Parker's restaurant opened in 1854. In an age when competent cooks earned eight dollars a week, Mr. Parker paid his chef, a Frenchman by the name of Sanzian, a staggering $5,000 a year for his culinary talents. During Sanzian's reign, many Parker House classics first appeared on the menu—Parker's tripes, Boston scrod (supposedly named for Mr. Scrod, one of the hotel's early managers), Boston cream pie—but it was a German baker named Ward who made Parker's a household word with the invention of the moist Parker House rolls. Dozens of nineteenth-century notables, including Dickens, Thackery, Emerson, Hawthorne, Longfellow and Sara Bernhardt, frequented the Parker House. The prestigious *Atlantic Monthly* was launched from one of Parker's private dining rooms in 1857.

The Parker House Hotel was completely rebuilt on its present site in 1925. Five years ago, Parker's dining room received a million-dollar facelift. The sweeping hall seats 140 today and tie and jacket are de rigueur. Parker's bill of fare retains the flavor of the past in the time-honored Continental and New England specialties which appear on the menu. But Parker's also keeps apace with the '80s with its nouvelle cuisine offerings and stylish Sunday brunch.

"You've got to dedicate your whole life to this business," says executive chef Joseph Ribas, who works ninety hours a week in the kitchen. Born in Guarda, Portugal, Ribas has worked all over Europe and Latin America and brings an international flair to his cuisine at the Parker House. Ribas came to Parker's nine years ago; today he commands a kitchen brigade of forty. He delights in the richness of New England's sea fare and in the challenge of uniting Parker's past and future in his cuisine.

TREMONT AND SCHOOL STREETS
BOSTON

PARKER HOUSE ROLLS

These rolls are the most famous dish on our menu. They were invented by the German baker named Ward in the middle of the last century. There was once a time when we would ship Parker House rolls daily to New York and even as far as Philadelphia.

This recipe makes 24 rolls.

½ cup scalded milk
½ cup boiling water
1 teaspoon salt
1 teaspoon sugar
5 tablespoons melted butter (approximately)
½ cake yeast dissolved in ¼ cup lukewarm water
3 cups bread flour (approximately)

1. Place milk, water, salt, sugar and 1 tablespoon butter into a bowl and mix well. Leave to cool slightly.
2. When the mixture is lukewarm, add yeast and stir in enough flour to obtain a thickish dough which you can knead. Knead well, then leave the dough to rise 1 hour or until doubled in bulk.
3. Shape dough into 1" balls and place on a buttered baking sheet and cover. When the balls have risen to double in bulk, press down in the center with the floured handle of a wooden spoon.
4. Brush one half of each roll liberally with butter and fold the other half over, pressing to form a small pocketbook.
5. Preheat oven to 350°.
6. Let the rolls rise again for 15 to 20 minutes or until doubled in bulk and bake for 12 to 15 minutes.
7. Brush the tops of the rolls with more butter after baking and serve warm.

A chef must have creativity, otherwise he will not succeed. You cannot be an eight-hour chef. I work fourteen to sixteen hours a day, six days a week. There are times when I go five weeks straight without a day off.

WARM MARINATED MUSSELS

The best mussels are the ones you pick right off the rocks among the seaweed. I would not suggest using the cultivated mussels—they don't have as much flavor. . . . To get rid of the sand, soak the mussels in a gallon of cold, salted water with a handful of corn meal for a day. The mussels eat the corn meal and spit out the sand.

32 mussels
2 tablespoons finely minced shallots
1 clove garlic, minced
1 tablespoon whole black peppercorns
3 tablespoons butter
¾ cup dry white wine
¾ cup **Fish Velouté**
½ cup heavy cream
Juice of ½ lemon
Dash of Worcestershire sauce
Salt and pepper

1. Thoroughly scrub the mussels and remove threads, discarding any mussels which fail to close when tapped.
2. Lightly sauté the shallots, garlic and peppercorns in butter. Add the mussels, wine and **Fish Velouté**. Simmer until the mussels open. Transfer mussels to a platter and keep warm.
3. Add the cream and simmer the sauce for 5 minutes or until slightly reduced and thickened.
4. Add lemon juice, Worcestershire sauce and salt and pepper to taste. Strain the sauce over the mussels and serve immediately.

Fish Velouté

1 pound white fish bones, thoroughly rinsed
1 small onion
1 rib celery
1 tablespoon chopped shallots
1 teaspoon black peppercorns
1 cup dry white wine
3 cups water
6 tablespoons butter
6 tablespoons flour
Salt and pepper to taste
Lemon juice to taste

1. Place fish bones, onion, celery, shallots, peppercorns, wine and water in a saucepan and gradually bring to boil.
2. Skim fish stock, reduce heat and gently simmer for 30 minutes.
3. Melt butter in a separate saucepan and whisk in the flour. Cook this mixture for 3 minutes, but do not let brown.
4. When the fish stock is ready, strain it into the flour mixture, whisking steadily.
5. Simmer for 30 minutes, correcting the seasoning with salt, pepper and lemon juice before using.

Note: It is not practical to make **Fish Velouté** in quantities less than 4 cups. The excess sauce here makes a delicious accompaniment for any seafood dish and can be frozen.

You have to have a feeling for the clientele. There are certain dishes which I would like to do, but the public just won't buy them. It's important to work closely with the maître d', to find out what people like.

MEDAILLONS DE VEAU CRESSONNIERE

When you go to buy veal, look at the color. The whiter the meat, the better the veal. Good veal should be tender, not stringy. The best veal is milk-fed veal—once the calf starts to eat grass, the color of the meat darkens. It becomes tough and you want to avoid it. . . . I slightly undercook my veal—I have always done that. The veal should never get browned when you cook it. To keep your veal nice and white, never overheat your frying pan.

¼ cup unsalted butter
8 (3-ounce) medallions, cut from the loin or tenderloin
1 carrot, diced
1 small onion, diced
2 ribs celery, diced
1 tablespoon minced shallots
1 teaspoon black peppercorns
1 cup dry white wine
1 large bunch watercress, leaves and stems separated (reserve stems)
2 cups heavy cream
1 cup unsalted butter at room temperature
Salt and pepper
Lemon juice to taste

1. Melt ¼ cup butter and gently sauté the veal medallions 4 to 5 minutes per side. Do not brown. When the medallions are cooked, or nearly cooked, transfer to a platter and keep warm.
2. Place the carrot, onion, celery, shallots, peppercorns, wine and watercress stems in the pan and simmer until the wine is reduced to about ¼ cup. Add the cream and continue simmering until ½ cup liquid remains.
3. Working off direct heat, but over a warm spot on the stove, gradually whisk in 1 cup unsalted butter to make a thick, silky sauce. This should take about 5 minutes. You can warm the sauce over a low heat, but if it boils, it will separate.
4. Strain the sauce and correct the seasoning with salt, pepper and lemon juice.
5. Add the watercress leaves to the hot sauce and spoon over the veal medallions. Serve at once.

People are getting away from the rich French sauces. Roux are out—the new sauces are made with wine or stock reductions—just like your mother used to do it at home. We were one of the first Boston restaurants to put nouvelle cuisine selections on our menu—they've been extremely popular.

HEARTS OF PALM VINAIGRETTE

1 large can hearts of palm
1 head Boston lettuce
1 tomato, sliced in wedges
4 thin slices red onion
¼ cup chopped parsley
4 lemon wedges
Vinaigrette Sauce

1. Quarter the larger hearts of palm lengthwise, leaving the smaller ones whole, and arrange on lettuce on 4 chilled salad plates. Garnish with tomato, onion, parsley and lemon wedges.
2. Pour **Vinaigrette Sauce** over the hearts of palm 5 minutes before serving.

Vinaigrette Sauce

1 teaspoon freshly chopped red onion
1 red pimiento
1 teaspoon chopped fresh tarragon
1 teaspoon chopped parsley
1 tablespoon lemon juice
¼ cup olive oil
1 tablespoon red wine vinegar
Dash of Worcestershire sauce
Salt and white pepper

Purée all ingredients in a blender.

STRAWBERRIES ROMANOFF

¾ cup heavy cream
2 pints strawberries, washed and hulled
½ cup Grand Marnier or other orange liqueur
2 tablespoons confectioners' sugar

1. Whip the heavy cream until it forms soft peaks.
2. Fold the strawberries into the cream.
3. Sprinkle orange liqueur and confectioners' sugar over the
   strawberries and serve in saucer-shaped champagne glasses.

*Cooking today is not like in the old days. When I took my apprentice-
ship in Portugal, if I did something wrong, my chef would slap me across
the face. He would make me wash pots for four days straight, without
doing anything else. Thank goodness those days are passed. Today a
chef has to be a teacher and a counselor.*

Dinner for Six

Catherine's Stallion

Pear Soup with Indonesian Hot Pepper Butter

Trout with Leeks and Raspberry Vinegar

Rice Pilaf

Stir-Fried Romaine, Watercress and Mushrooms

Chocolate, Chocolate, Chocolate

Wine:

With Pear Soup—Gewürtztraminer Vendage Tardive
(Rènè Schmidt) 1976
With Trout—Beaujolais Villages (Cellier de la Barre)
1978

Christopher Evans, Proprietor and Chef

"My mother was the world's worst cook," Marblehead restaurateur Christopher Evans remarks with a smile. But she did introduce Chris to the potential of the cuisine of Germany. It was not until Chris, at the time a disenchanted theology student, met cooking instructor Madeleine Kamman that the dream of opening a restaurant of his own emerged. In January of 1979 the Felix Krull opened its doors in Chandler's Row in Marblehead and he has been delighting Bay Staters with its unique blend of ethnic cooking and nouvelle cuisine ever since.

"We don't pretend to cook Germanic food," says Evans, "but we do play with many of the flavor combinations—caraway, horseradish, smoked meats, eaux de vie—indigenous to central Europe. Our sauces, on the other hand, which are based on reductions of wine, stock or vinegar and enriched with butter and cream instead of the traditional flour thickeners, are strictly nouvelle cuisine." In the quest for new flavor combinations, Christopher Evans and company have gone through 300 recipes in the course of the past year. "When a lot of people first ate at our restaurant, they complained that the food was too complicated," says Evans. "We rarely work with more than five or six major ingredients—to my mind, we're really very simple."

Although a serious chef, Christopher Evans has an irrepressible sense of humor. He named the Felix Krull after a character in a Thomas Mann novel, who, according to the menu, through "hard work, tact and discretion" became one of the top maître d's in Europe. "It took exactly two restaurant reviews to break the secret that Krull was also one of the greatest con artists in Western literature," recalls Chris with a chuckle. A meat dish on the menu bears the name of Krull's notorious mistress; a cocktail recalls Catherine the Great's equine paramour. A dessert of dark chocolate ice cream with white chocolate chips plays intriguing tricks with diners' expectations.

"The original décor was too stark for the local suburban clientele," says Chris, "so we've added some prints and some color to the place." The stylish, second-floor restaurant seats forty and does a brisk brunch trade in the summer. Guests dine off fine Villeroy china.

CHANDLER'S ROW, 3 SPRING STREET
MARBLEHEAD

CATHERINE'S STALLION

In memory of the late Empress's trusty steed. This cocktail is an invention of M.L. Redmon and myself when we were students at the Modern Gourmet. Two of these laid us low. The name is a raunchy suggestion that stuck.

12 ounces vodka
2 tablespoons crème de cassis
1½ to 2 quarts Gerolsteiner or other sparkling water

1. Place 2 ounces vodka and 1 teaspoon crème de cassis in each of 6 highball glasses and fill with ice.
2. Add sparkling water to taste.

The most important quality for a chef is patience—patience to do research, patience to see things through. I have seen people who work for me try to slam a dish together in ten minutes that really requires one hour. It just won't work.

PEAR SOUP WITH INDONESIAN HOT PEPPER BUTTER

One day my produce man handed me a jar of Indonesian hot pepper paste and said, "Chris, I want you to give this a try." That's how this dish came to be. . . . Indonesian hot pepper paste, sometimes called Sambal Ulek, is available in gourmet shops and some Chinese grocery stores. I suppose you could substitute Hungarian paprika paste, which comes in tubes.

½ pound shallots, peeled and chopped
2 large onions, chopped
¾ cup unsalted butter
4 ripe Anjou or Bartlett pears, peeled, cored and sliced
1 quart chicken stock
1 pint heavy cream
Salt and freshly ground black pepper
Lemon juice to taste
2 tablespoons Indonesian red pepper paste (Sambal Ulek)

1. Gently sauté the shallots and onions in ¼ cup butter in an enamel or stainless steel saucepan. Cook until translucent, but do not let brown.
2. Add the pears and stock and bring soup to a boil. Reduce heat and gently simmer for 1 to 1½ hours or until the flavors are well concentrated.
3. Purée the soup in a food processor or blender; strain. Add the cream to the purée and season with salt, pepper and lemon juice to taste. (The soup may be prepared well in advance to this point and simply reheated before serving.)
4. To prepare the butter garnish, whip the remaining ½ cup butter with the pepper paste and season with salt and lemon juice. The pepper butter should be spicy enough to produce a good contrast with the mellowness of the pears.
5. For serving, swirl a spoonful of pepper butter in each individual bowl of hot soup.

Note: This soup can also be served cold in the summertime. To make the pepper garnish, substitute sour cream for the butter.

TROUT WITH LEEKS AND RASPBERRY VINEGAR

Raspberry leaves are often available in health and natural food stores. Raspberry vinegar is available in fancy gourmet shops at outrageous prices. It can be produced easily and much less expensively by infusing cider or wine vinegar with defrosted and drained frozen raspberries, or even with the seeds and pulp from strained raspberry purée. The longer the infusion stands in a cool, dark place, the better it will taste.

6 fresh brook trout, boned (leave heads and tails intact)
Salt and pepper
1 bunch leeks, washed, the white portion julienned (cut into 2"
  matchsticks), the green tops saved for the wine reduction
2 cups red Côtes du Rhône wine
2 cups **Fish Fumet**
⅓ cup raspberry vinegar
1 onion, sliced
1 tablespoon thyme
8 sprigs parsley
1 bay leaf
3 tablespoons raspberry leaves
1½ pints heavy cream
1 tablespoon cornstarch
Lemon juice to taste
¼ cup chopped parsley

1. Season the trout cavities with salt and pepper.
2. Blanch the leek bottoms in boiling, salted water for 1 minute. Rinse in cold water and stuff the trout cavities.
3. Combine the wine, 1¾ cups **Fish Fumet**, vinegar, onion and herbs in an enamel or stainless steel saucepan. Bring to a boil, lower heat and simmer mixture until there are only 1½ cups remaining. Reduce the heavy cream by a third over a low heat. Strain the wine reduction into the cream.
4. Mix the cornstarch with the remaining ¼ cup **Fish Fumet** and whisk it gradually into the cream sauce. Whisking constantly, bring the sauce to a boil to thicken, then season to taste with salt, pepper and lemon juice. Keep warm.

continued

5. Preheat oven to 375°.
6. Wrap trout in individual tin foil pouches and bake for 5 to 7 minutes or until firm to the touch.
7. Arrange trout on a platter. Spoon sauce over it and sprinkle with chopped parsley.

A reduction is simply a gradual boiling down of a liquid to concentrate the flavor. We will reduce vinegar four or five times for our vinegar sauces.

Fish Fumet

This makes four cups. Use extra for pilaf.

2 pounds fish heads and bones (use bones from white fish, like
    sole, haddock or halibut)
1 onion, peeled and quartered
1 small carrot, diced
Bouquet garni of bay leaf, thyme and parsley
10 peppercorns
Water to cover (about 1 quart)

Combine all ingredients in a saucepan and heat almost to boiling. Reduce flame and gently simmer for 25 minutes, skimming the surface from time to time to remove any foam. Strain before using.

Finishing the sauce is the hardest part about cooking. You must attain a perfect balance between the acidity, the salt and the pepper— making sure that the taste of the raspberry comes through and that the flavor of the leek is there too. This balancing act is always the most difficult part in cooking—that's all that cooking is, in fact, a balancing act—playing one ingredient off against the other.

RICE PILAF

1 onion, finely chopped
¼ cup unsalted butter
1 cup uncooked long-grain rice
2 cups boiling **Fish Fumet**
Salt and pepper

1. Preheat the oven to 400°.
2. Sauté the onion in butter in a cast-iron pan until soft. Add the rice and continue to sauté for 4 to 5 minutes or until the rice begins to turn translucent.
3. Add the **Fish Fumet** and seasonings and tightly cover the pan.
4. Bake in preheated oven for 20 minutes. Remove from oven and fluff with a fork before serving.

Our stock is made of veal bones, veal breast, leeks, onions, carrots and herbs. We let it cook for eighteen to twenty hours—by that time it has taken on a very good color and delicious flavor. It's very versatile.

STIR-FRIED ROMAINE, WATERCRESS AND MUSHROOMS

¼ cup unsalted butter
¼ pound mushrooms, washed and thinly sliced
1 head romaine lettuce, washed, dried and cut into ½" strips
1 bunch watercress, washed and coarse stems removed
Salt and freshly ground black pepper

1. Melt butter in a skillet. Briskly sauté the mushrooms for 3 minutes.
2. Add the romaine lettuce and sauté for 2 more minutes.
3. Add the watercress and sauté for 1 minute. Season to taste before serving.

You can get more flavor from butter sauces than you can from perfectly executed flour sauces. We use virtually no flour in our cooking.

CHOCOLATE, CHOCOLATE, CHOCOLATE

12 ounces bittersweet chocolate
6 egg yolks
$\frac{2}{3}$ cup sugar
$\frac{1}{4}$ teaspoon salt
1 cup light cream
$2\frac{1}{4}$ cups heavy cream
1 tablespoon vanilla extract
3 ounces white chocolate, coarsely chopped
Bittersweet chocolate liqueur

1. Melt 6 ounces bittersweet chocolate over a bowl of hot water.
2. Whisk the yolks, sugar and salt together until mixed but not foamy. Add light cream and 2 cups heavy cream. Poach the mixture in a heavy-bottomed saucepan over a low heat for a few minutes to make a crème anglaise (custard sauce). When the steam starts to rise, the foam subsides to small bubbles and the mixture coats the back of a wooden spoon, the crème is cooked. Do not let the mixture boil, or it will curdle.
3. Stir until cooled and add the vanilla and melted chocolate.
4. Once the mixture has cooled, churn in an ice-cream machine until beginning to set, or harden the mixture in a bowl in the freezer, whisking repeatedly during the freezing process to break up the ice crystals.
5. When the cream starts to thicken, add the white chocolate chips and continue freezing. When solid, scoop out balls of ice cream and place in the freezer. Allow for 2 scoops per serving.
6. Melt the remaining bittersweet chocolate in $\frac{1}{4}$ cup heavy cream and cool it as much as possible, still keeping it fluid. Spear each scoop of ice cream with a fork and dip it into the tepid chocolate. Return to freezer.
7. To serve, place 2 ice-cream balls in a glass bowl and pour chocolate liqueur around the bottom.

There are dishes we put on our menu which we have never tried before. It may seem risky, but we have enough confidence in ourselves that, within certain limits, they'll work.

Dinner for Four

Mushroom and Crab Strudel

Roast Cornish Game Hens with Lemon-Cumin Butter

Bibb Lettuce Salad with Pecan Vinaigrette

Almond Cream Peach Tart

Wine:

*With Strudel and Dessert—Joseph Perrier Champagne
Cuvée Royale 1973
With Entrée—Spring Mountain California
Chardonnay 1977*

*Ben and Jane Thompson, Proprietors
Frank McClelland, Chef*

Most people know Ben Thompson as the architect who redesigned the Faneuil Hall Marketplace. The same aesthetic excitement pervades Thompson's thriving Harvard Square eating establishment, the Harvest. Bright Marimekko fabrics (which Thompson introduced to the United States from Finland) and colorful food prints festoon the 180-seat restaurant/terrace café/nightspot. The entire dining room color scheme shifts twice yearly, green to brown to green, suggesting the eternal planting and harvesting cycles.

But the visual is only part of the Harvest dining experience and guests flock here for a cuisine which intrigues the palate, as the décor excites the eye. The Harvest may be the only restaurant in New England which serves leg of lion, llama loin, whole wild boar, suckling pig and haunch of elephant—all roasted over coals on the terrace. Even in the more conventional dishes, a spirit of innovation reigns. "We want people to be able to get something different, something out of the ordinary at the Harvest," says restaurant manager Alice Bailey. "Our cooks know all the basics, but they strive to take Continental cuisine one step farther."

Bailey describes the Harvest as a family restaurant, although the employees are not actually related. "Thanks to our Harvard Square location, we attract lots of enthusiastic young people who are eager to learn how to cook." Every week the Harvest organizes special food seminars for its employees. "Most of our people attend, though they don't get paid for it," says Bailey. "They're just interested—the Harvest is that kind of place."

44 BRATTLE STREET
CAMBRIDGE

MUSHROOM AND CRAB STRUDEL

5 tablespoons butter
½ medium onion, chopped
12 ounces fresh mushrooms, washed and thinly sliced
5 ounces crab meat
3 tablespoons heavy cream
1 teaspoon arrowroot or cornstarch
2 tablespoons Madeira
Splash of Worcestershire sauce
Salt and cayenne pepper
5 sheets of filo dough
¼ cup dried bread crumbs

1. Preheat oven to 400°.
2. Melt 2 tablespoons butter in a shallow pan and sauté the onion until soft and transparent. Add the mushrooms and sauté for 5 minutes. Dice the crab meat into the pan and add the cream. Simmer for 1 minute.
3. Dissolve the arrowroot in the Madeira and stir it into the crab mixture. Simmer for 2 minutes, then season with Worcestershire sauce, salt and cayenne.
4. Melt the remaining butter. Carefully remove the filo dough from the package and stack on the work surface.
5. Brush the top sheet with melted butter and sprinkle with bread crumbs. Spread the mushroom-crab mixture along the bottom edge and roll around the stuffing to make a compact cylinder. Butter the second sheet of filo dough, sprinkle with more bread crumbs and roll around the crab cylinder. Repeat the process with the remaining filo, butter and bread crumbs.
6. Bake in preheated oven for 18 minutes. Slice in fourths and serve.

Note: Filo dough—sold in 1-pound packages of paper-thin sheets— is available in any Greek or Armenian grocery store and in the frozen gourmet food sections of many supermarkets as well.

When our chef tastes a dish, he knows exactly what it needs to bring out every little subtlety. He's a fine-tuner.

ROAST CORNISH GAME HENS WITH LEMON-CUMIN BUTTER

4 fresh Cornish game hens
2 cups unsalted butter at room temperature
1½ tablespoons ground cumin
Juice of 1 large lemon
1 teaspoon Worcestershire sauce
Pinch of cayenne pepper
Salt to taste

1. Preheat oven to 425°.
2. Rinse off the hens and pat dry.
3. Cream the butter and beat in the remaining ingredients.
4. To prepare the birds for stuffing, gently loosen the skin from the meat with your fingers. Spread the spiced butter under the skin, quite liberally around the breast area, reserving one-fourth for the outside of the bird. Truss the hens, sprinkle with salt and smear with the remaining butter.
5. Roast the birds in preheated oven for 25 minutes or until the juices from the thigh run clear, basting often with the fat which accumulates in the roasting pan. Serve with rice pilaf or buttered noodles.

The secret to fine cuisine is good ingredients. I spend at least an hour a day on the telephone with my purveyors. I push them hard to supply me with what's freshest and best.

The first time I came to the Harvest, I saw the chef cooking a wild boar on the garden terrace. That alone convinced me I wanted to work here.

BIBB LETTUCE SALAD WITH PECAN VINAIGRETTE

1 head Bibb lettuce
1 whole egg
1½ teaspoons Dijon-style mustard
1 cup vegetable oil
Juice of ½ lemon
Grated rind of ½ lemon, blanched in boiling water for 1 minute,
    rinsed and drained
Pinch of tarragon leaves (fresh if possible)
1½ tablespoons tarragon vinegar
1 tablespoon honey
½ cup finely chopped pecans
Salt and pepper

1. Separate and wash lettuce leaves. Dry.
2. Whisk the egg with the mustard. Gradually whisk in the oil in a
   thin stream, followed by the remaining ingredients. Season to taste.
3. Toss the lettuce with the pecan vinaigrette and serve on chilled
   salad plates.

Note: The dressing can be whisked by hand or made in a blender
or food processor. If using the latter, be careful not to overbeat.

*We make everything from scratch at the Harvest. All our sauces are
made to order. All our vegetables are cooked to order. We have fresh
produce delivery six days a week.*

ALMOND CREAM PEACH TART

Pâte Royale
Almond Cream
Pastry Cream
10 to 12 fresh peaches

1. Preheat oven to 425°.
2. Line a 9" flan ring or French tart pan with the **Pâte Royale**. Combine the **Almond Cream** with the cooled **Pastry Cream** and spoon the mixture into the pie shell.
3. Plunge the peaches into boiling water for 30 seconds, then rinse under cold water. Remove the skins and slice each peach into 8 wedges. Arrange the peach slices on top of the filling in a decorative pattern.
4. Bake in preheated oven for 25 to 30 minutes or until the almond filling is puffed and browned.

Pâte Royale

2 cups all-purpose flour
1 teaspoon salt
1½ teaspoons sugar
1 cup unsalted butter
2 egg yolks
3 tablespoons heavy cream

1. Sift the flour onto a work surface and make a well in the center. Place the remaining ingredients in the well.
2. Mix the liquid ingredients with the fingertips, gradually incorporating the flour, and knead with the heel of the palm to obtain a smooth dough. Work the dough as little as possible.
3. Chill the dough for at least 30 minutes before rolling it out.

Almond Cream

6 tablespoons unsalted butter at room temperature
⅔ cup ground almonds
⅔ cup confectioners' sugar
1 egg
2 teaspoons Myers's rum
1 tablespoon cornstarch

Cream the butter and beat in the almonds and sugar. When the mixture is well mixed, whisk in the egg. Beat in the rum and cornstarch, whisking until the mixture is light and smooth.

Pastry Cream

½ cup milk
Small piece of lemon peel
Few drops of vanilla extract
2 egg yolks
¼ cup sugar
2 tablespoons flour
1 tablespoon butter

1. Scald the milk with the lemon peel and vanilla.
2. Whisk together the yolks, sugar and flour.
3. Pour the boiling milk into the yolk mixture, whisking constantly, and return the mixture to the saucepan. Boil vigorously for 3 minutes, stirring continuously to prevent scorching.
4. Remove from heat, dot with butter and leave to cool.

Hermitage

Dinner for Six

Cream of Horseradish Soup

Grilled Swordfish with Lime, Parsley and Garlic

Rock Cornish Game Hen "Tabaka" with Tkemali Sauce

Gratin of Beet Greens

Chestnut Mousse

Wine:

With Soup and First Course—Deutz Champagne NV
With Game Hen—Red Hermitage (Guigal) 1972

Rafael Pons and Leo Romero, Proprietors

The Brahmin dining establishment arched its eyebrows when a pair of Cuban entrepreneurs decided to open the Bay State's first and only gourmet Russian restaurant. Boston *becs fins* quickly learned, however, that there was far more to the cuisine of Imperial Russia than the ubiquitous borscht and black bread and that one need not be Soviet to prepare it. The unusual locale—the former 16th Precinct police station—only enhances the unique dining experience at one of the most touted restaurants in the Back Bay.

Since it opened in 1975, the Hermitage has shared its massive Boylston Street brownstone with the Institute of Contemporary Arts. As exhibits change in the museum upstairs, new prints and canvases decorate the cool brown walls of the restaurant. A cloth and wood assemblage commissioned by the Hermitage's owners hangs over the two-tiered dining area, evoking the awnings of a central European café and the tents of a Russian circus.

"Most people think that Russian food is heavy and overbearing," observes owner Rafael Pons, "that you have to drink lots of vodka and be very cold to enjoy it." Nothing could be further from the fare served at the Hermitage. "We take our inspiration from the Russians, but our cooking techniques from the nouvelle cuisine chefs of France," says Rafael. "We use less sour cream than the Soviets and don't cook with any flour in our sauces. As a result, guests can enjoy a substantial meal without being overburdened by the heaviness of the food."

Rafael Pons smiles when asked how a Cuban, who has never set foot in the Soviet Union, can presume to serve authentic fare in his restaurant. "We are not trying to cook as though we were in Russia," he says. "We wish to preserve the flavor and spicing of Russian cuisine in a form which is palatable for Americans."

"Where else can a cook combine the flavors of France, Germany, the Balkans and even Asia?" exclaims a young Hermitage chef. "The cuisine at the Hermitage is every chef's dream!"

955 BOYLSTON STREET
BOSTON

CREAM OF HORSERADISH SOUP

1 cup dried navy beans or Great Northern white beans
6 cups cold water
5 cups milk
½ cup chopped shallots
3 tablespoons prepared white horseradish or to taste
Salt and pepper
1 cup dry white wine
1½ cups heavy cream
6 thin slices lemon

1. Cover the beans with the cold water and gradually bring to a boil. Cover pot and simmer gently for 1 hour. Drain beans.
2. Scald the milk, add beans and chopped shallots and simmer over low heat for 10 to 15 minutes or until the beans are very tender.
3. Purée this mixture in a blender or food processor and strain through a fine sieve. Whisk in the horseradish, salt and pepper.
4. In a separate saucepan, boil the white wine until reduced by half. Add the heavy cream and continue boiling until only 1 cup liquid remains. Stir this into the bean-horseradish mixture and season again to taste.
5. To serve, warm the soup slowly and garnish each full soup bowl with a lemon slice.

The person in charge of a restaurant must have a great deal of freedom. We don't try to dictate the way something must be done here. A great deal of experimentation goes on in the Hermitage kitchen.

GRILLED SWORDFISH WITH LIME, PARSLEY AND GARLIC

*Remove the zest—outer skin—of the lime with a vegetable peeler.
This leaves the bitter white pith behind. . . . When crushing garlic,
always mash the clove with the salt. The garlic will pulverize evenly
and the salt will absorb the juice. . . . The swordfish can be served as
shish kebab instead of in steaks. Cut the fish into one-inch cubes
and grill it on skewers.*

5 to 6 cloves garlic, peeled
Salt and freshly ground black pepper
1 cup vegetable oil
Juice of 2 fresh lemons
Juice and zest of 4 large limes
½ bunch parsley, finely chopped
1½ pounds fresh swordfish
1 lime, thinly sliced

1. Mash the garlic with salt and add the oil, lemon juice, lime juice and
   zest, parsley and pepper. Let sit in a shallow earthenware dish for
   1 hour.
2. Remove the skin from the swordfish and cut into 6 even-sized steaks.
   Place the fish in the marinade and marinate overnight in the
   refrigerator or for 3 to 4 hours at room temperature. Pour off the
   marinade and reserve.
3. Preheat the grill or broiler and cook the swordfish 4 to 5 minutes per
   side, basting with the reserved marinade. Garnish fish with fresh lime
   slices for serving.

*The way I learned to cook was, quite simply, to start cooking. I made
some horrendous mistakes at first. It really helps to be thrown into
the middle of a busy kitchen, like the peasant child whose parents
toss him into the Volga to teach him how to swim.*

ROCK CORNISH GAME HEN "TABAKA" WITH TKEMALI SAUCE

The people of Georgia (the south-central region of Russia between the Black and Caspian seas) are particularly fond of combining fruits and meats. The tabaka—*meat marinated in spiced orange juice—is typical of Georgian fare. Traditionally, the game hens are roasted whole on a spit, but we prefer to bone the fowls completely for a more enjoyable, elegant dining experience.*

6 Rock Cornish game hens
Marinade
1 cup clarified butter
6 cups peanut oil
1 orange, thinly sliced
1 scallion, finely chopped
Tkemali Sauce

1. Bone the Cornish game hens, leaving only the wing bones intact (or have your butcher do it). The fowls should assume a flat, rectangular shape when boned. Place hens in **Marinade** and marinate overnight in the refrigerator or for 6 hours at room temperature, turning from time to time to assure even flavoring. Remove hens and blot dry on a clean dish towel.
2. Heat the clarified butter and 2 cups oil in a shallow sauté pan large enough to hold 2 hens side by side. When the fat is almost smoking, lower 2 hens skin side down into the pan, holding the wings and legs in separate hands. (Be very careful. The fat will foam and splutter when it comes in contact with the bird.) Place a pot lid or heavy metal pie pan on top of the birds to flatten them. Cook for 5 minutes, gently shaking the pan from time to time to prevent sticking and assure that the hens cook evenly. When the skin side has thoroughly browned, turn the birds with tongs and replace the weight. Lower heat and continue frying for 5 minutes or until the thighs are cooked (the juices will run clear when the bird is pricked with a skewer). Remove hens, drain and keep warm. Cook the remaining hens as described above, adding additional oil with each batch.
3. For serving, garnish with fresh orange slices and chopped scallions, with a dab of **Tkemali Sauce** on the side.

Marinade

1 cup orange juice concentrate
1 cup peanut oil
½ cup dry white wine
2 cloves garlic, crushed
5 to 6 shallots, peeled and minced
1 (3") slice fresh ginger, peeled
2 teaspoons salt
2 teaspoons Hungarian paprika
½ teaspoon freshly grated nutmeg
3 sticks cinnamon
½ teaspoon cayenne pepper
Pinch of ground allspice
1 teaspoon granulated sugar
1 thick slice lemon

Combine all ingredients in a shallow, nonaluminum pan and let sit at room temperature for 1 hour. The mixture should have a brown hue and a very intense flavor.

Tkemali Sauce

1 small clove garlic, minced
½ teaspoon ground coriander
3 tablespoons hot water
½ cup Japanese Umeboshi plum paste (or enough whole sour plums to
    make ½ cup paste following the method described below)
3 tablespoons peanut oil

Beat the garlic, coriander and hot water into the plum paste. Gradually beat in the oil and chill. Remove from the refrigerator shortly before serving.

Georgians serve grilled meats with a tart relish called tkemali, made with special sour plums which grow in the region. To approximate the sauce in this country, we use salted Umeboshi plums, available in any Japanese market. To make Umeboshi plum paste, soak whole plums in boiling water to soften, then slip out the seeds and mash the flesh with a fork. Tkemali Sauce is very concentrated—a small dab will sauce a whole portion of meat. Leftover sauce will keep almost indefinitely in the freezer.

GRATIN OF BEET GREENS

2 to 3 pounds beet greens, thoroughly washed and dried
½ cup pot or farmer's cheese
1 clove garlic, mashed
6 tablespoons unsalted butter
1 pound mushrooms, washed and thinly sliced
3 egg yolks
3 tablespoons finely chopped shallots
Salt and pepper
½ cup dried bread crumbs
¼ cup freshly grated Parmesan cheese

1. Preheat oven to 350°.
2. Chop the beet greens coarsely.
3. Force the pot cheese through a fine-meshed sieve.
4. Sauté the garlic gently in 2 tablespoons butter, being careful not to brown. Add the sliced mushrooms and gently sauté for 5 minutes. Remove from heat.
5. Heat 2 tablespoons butter in a second sauté pan and add the beet greens. Cook over high heat for 3 minutes or until the leaves wilt and most of the water evaporates. Cool.
6. Whisk the pot cheese with the egg yolks, adding the chopped shallots, salt and pepper. Stir in the cooled beet greens and mushrooms and spread the mixture evenly in a buttered baking dish.
7. Sprinkle the top with the bread crumbs and Parmesan cheese and dot with the remaining butter. (The gratin can be prepared ahead of time to this stage.)
8. Bake in preheated oven for 35 to 40 minutes or until the mixture has set. Serve at once.

CHESTNUT MOUSSE

The sweetness of this chestnut mousse can be varied to suit your taste. Mashed fresh chestnuts or unsweetened chestnut purée will require more sugar than the sweetened purée generally sold in markets.

4 eggs, separated and at room temperature
½ to 1 cup brown or white sugar
1 teaspoon vanilla extract
¼ cup good Cognac
3 tablespoons unsalted butter
1 (4-ounce) can chestnut purée
½ teaspoon almond extract
½ teaspoon cream of tartar
3 tablespoons white sugar
1½ cups well-chilled heavy cream
6 tablespoons toasted, slivered almonds

1. Whisk the egg yolks with the ½ to 1 cup brown or white sugar. Beat in the vanilla and half the Cognac.
2. Cook the yolk mixture over a pan of hot water on low heat for a few minutes, stirring gently with a wooden spoon. When the mixture begins to thicken, start beating with a whisk and beat until the yolks are light and moussey. Remove from heat, dot with butter to prevent a skin from forming and leave the yolks to cool.
3. Add the remaining Cognac to the chestnut purée. Stir the yolk mixture to incorporate the butter and fold it into the chestnut purée. Add the almond extract and leave the mixture until completely cooled.
4. Beat the egg whites by hand or by machine in a grease-free stainless steel or copper bowl. Start beating slowly to break up the egg whites, then add the cream of tartar. Increase speed and beat until whites are firm. Sprinkle in the 3 tablespoons white sugar and continue beating until completely stiff and glossy.
5. Whip the heavy cream until it holds stiff peaks.
6. Stir a quarter of the egg whites into the chestnut mixture to lighten it, then gently fold in the remaining whites.
7. Fold in the whipped cream, reserving ½ cup cream for garnish.
8. Spoon into serving cups and chill for at least 3 hours before serving. To serve, pipe rosettes of whipped cream on the top of each mousse and sprinkle with toasted almonds.

You have to master cooking techniques so well that they become second nature to you. Then and only then can you express yourself in your cooking. . . . There's nothing reprehensible about being a great technician. But if you are going to get involved with the dialectic of cooking, you have to make it a personal experience.

People don't come to this restaurant for a perfect reconstruction of what was or is served at the Russian table. They dine here because they trust the chef's talents and creative abilities. We presuppose the right to translate Russian cuisine to our own and our customers' tastes.

I don't want professional waiters working here. I want young people, fresh people, who take pride in what they are doing and in the food they serve. Our waiters are our worst critics—when a dish or sauce is not right, they let us know about it.

LE BOCAGE

Dinner for Six

Shrimp and Cape Scallops Rémoulade

Fennel Soup

Rack of Lamb with Poivrade Sauce

Gratin Dauphinoise

Pineapple with Rum

Wine:

With First Course and Soup—Champagne Brut NV
(Albert Larive)
With Lamb—Château Talbot 1967
After Dinner—Sandeman Port 1963

Enzo Danesi, Proprietor
Maurie Warren, Chef

"You can't learn the restaurant business in five years," says Enzo Danesi. As owner of the eminently successful Bocage restaurant in Watertown, he should know. Born near Milano, Italy, Enzo began his career forty years ago. He worked in France, Germany, Switzerland and Greece before coming to Boston. After being told by his doctor to "take it easy" six years ago, Enzo sold a booming eating establishment downtown to purchase a tiny Cambridge restaurant called Le Bocage.

"I always wanted a small place where I could do things right," muses Enzo. Within no time, crowds thronged to the Huron Avenue storefront. The success strained the tiny Bocage kitchen, forcing Enzo to move the restaurant to the more spacious site in Watertown that it occupies today.

Part of what makes Enzo's restaurant so popular is the "Bocage system," emulated by countless other eating establishments in the area. The Bocage's limited menu changes daily, assuring guests the freshest possible comestibles. The white walls and simple but tasteful décor—modeled after the country inns of Northern Italy—offer patrons comfortable dining without distraction. "My service is down to earth," says Enzo, who prefers college students to professional waiters. "They say 'good evening' and everyone feels at ease."

"My chef, Maurie Warren, came to me fresh out of cooking school and he always had his nose buried in cookbooks. One day I told him, 'You know the basics—forget the recipes and follow your own sense of taste and palate.' I tell you, Maurie's a great chef," says Enzo with paternal pride. "There isn't a guy like him in Boston."

72 BIGELOW AVENUE
WATERTOWN

SHRIMP AND CAPE SCALLOPS REMOULADE

We often run out of fish because I just buy the limit. I don't want anything to be left over for the next day.

24 large shrimp, peeled and deveined
Court Bouillon
1 pound Cape scallops, half-moon-shaped muscle on the side of the
    scallops removed
Lettuce leaves
Rémoulade Sauce
3 tablespoons finely chopped parsley
2 tablespoons whole capers

1. Place the shrimp in cool **Court Bouillon** and heat slowly to poach the shrimp. Do not boil. The shrimp will feel firm to the touch when cooked, but taste one to make sure. Remove with a slotted spoon and chill.
2. Cool the **Court Bouillon.** When cool, add the scallops and reheat slowly to gently poach until cooked. They should, if anything, remain a little under done. Drain scallops and transfer to a cool place to chill.
3. Line 6 small plates with lettuce leaves. Toss the seafood with the **Rémoulade Sauce** and mound in the center of the plates.
4. Sprinkle with parsley and capers before serving.

Court Bouillon

2 quarts cold water
2 tablespoons salt
1 onion, peeled and sliced
1 carrot, thinly sliced
Bouquet garni of bay leaf, thyme and parsley
10 whole peppercorns

1. Combine all ingredients in a large saucepan and simmer for 15 minutes.
2. Strain and cool.

Rémoulade Sauce

2 egg yolks
1 tablespoon Dijon-style mustard
Dash of vinegar
½ teaspoon salt
1⅓ cups vegetable oil
2 tablespoons olive oil
2 tablespoons red wine vinegar
1 small clove garlic, minced
1 anchovy filet, finely chopped
1 tablespoon minced onion
2 tablespoons capers, rinsed and finely chopped
2 tablespoons finely chopped parsley
Salt and freshly ground black pepper

1. Whisk the egg yolks, mustard, vinegar and salt in a heavy bowl or blender.
2. Gradually dribble in the oils, whisking continually, to make an emulsified mayonnaise.
3. Whisk in vinegar, garlic, anchovy, onion, capers and parsley and season to taste.

Our favorite olive oil is made by the Berio Co.; for vinegar we use Dessaux et Fils.

Most of the time I cook by look, smell and taste. Beware of pseudo-precision in recipes; it only gives you false confidence.

FENNEL SOUP

A good chef knows how to substitute. This soup could be made with zucchini, broccoli, lettuce—almost any ingredient. . . . Fennel is an aromatic herb in the parsley family. It looks vaguely like celery and has the taste and aroma of anise.

2 large leeks, trimmed, washed and sliced
2 bulbs fennel, thinly sliced, stalks and green leaves removed
1 small can imported Italian tomatoes
1 quart good homemade chicken stock
2 cups heavy cream
Salt and pepper

1. Place leeks, fennel, tomatoes and stock in a large pot and simmer for 1½ to 2 hours or until the vegetables are very tender.
2. Purée the soup in a blender and force through a fine sieve to remove vegetable threads and fibers. (A food processor does a very poor job on soups.)
3. Add the cream and salt and pepper to taste. The soup should have a distinct fennel flavor—if necessary, add a couple of splashes of Pernod.

I could not have opened a restaurant like Le Bocage twenty years ago. The Boston clientele was completely different—much more a steak and potatoes crowd.

I always tell people, if they want a good dinner, they should go to the restaurant on a week night, when the chef and waiter have time to do their jobs properly.

RACK OF LAMB WITH POIVRADE SAUCE

Lamb is a young animal, so the difference between Prime and Choice is not that great. There is good lamb and bad lamb, however, and you should look for a light color and "large eye" when you go to select your rack. Unless you're an experienced meatcutter, have your butcher trim off the fat.

3 racks of lamb, trimmed and oven-ready
6 tablespoons melted butter
Salt and pepper
Poivrade Sauce

1. Preheat oven to 425°.
2. Brush the lamb with melted butter, season with salt and pepper and roast for 20 minutes or until cooked to taste. (Rare lamb will read 120° on a meat thermometer, medium-rare lamb—the way we like to serve it—will read 125° to 130°.) Let the meat rest for a few minutes before carving into chops.
3. Serve with **Poivrade Sauce** and a nice vegetable.

Poivrade Sauce

4 pounds lamb bones and lamb trimmings (shanks, breasts and necks make good stock)
2 carrots, coarsely chopped
1 onion, peeled and quartered
1 whole head garlic, halved laterally
Bouquet garni of bay leaf, thyme and parsley
2½ quarts water
2 cups dry red wine
1 cup good red wine vinegar
1 carrot, finely chopped
1 onion, peeled and chopped
2 shallots, chopped
3 sprigs parsley
2 teaspoons cracked peppercorns
2 teaspoons potato starch
¼ cup Armagnac
1 to 2 teaspoons crème de cassis (red currant liqueur)
Salt and pepper

1. Preheat oven to 400°.
2. Roast bones for 1½ hours or until thoroughly browned. Drain off fat and transfer the bones to a stockpot with trimmings, coarsely chopped carrots, quartered onion, garlic, bouquet garni and water.
3. Bring to a boil, skim stock and reduce heat. Simmer for 5 hours, skimming from time to time to remove surface scum, adding more water as necessary to end up with 2 quarts lamb stock.
4. Strain into a saucepan, setting ¼ cup stock aside. Boil stock until reduced to about 2½ cups.
5. Place wine, vinegar, finely chopped carrot, chopped onion, shallots, parsley and cracked peppercorns in another saucepan and boil until reduced to about ½ cup.
6. Strain the wine reduction into the stock reduction and bring to a boil.
7. Dissolve the potato starch in the reserved ¼ cup lamb stock and whisk it into the boiling reduction to thicken.
8. Flame the Armagnac and add it to the sauce. Add the crème de cassis, which should impart a hint of fruit flavor to the sauce but not overpower it.
9. Correct the seasoning and strain the sauce through a fine sieve or cheesecloth before serving.

Note: You can use a good, homemade veal or chicken stock provided it's unsalted, but the flavor of the final sauce will not be the same. It always pays to keep a little extra stock on hand to adjust the sauce in case something does not go as planned.

Armagnac is a grape brandy made in the southwest of France. We prefer it to Cognac for this dish, because long aging in wood makes it more flavorful. We use La Vie Armagnac, which is exceptionally good for the price.

GRATIN DAUPHINOISE

This dish reheats well and should be cooked before the lamb goes into the oven.

4 Idaho potatoes, peeled and cut into ¼" thick slices
1 clove garlic, cut in half
¼ cup butter
Salt and pepper
Freshly grated nutmeg
1 cup heavy cream (approximately)

1. Place potato slices in cold, salted water to cover and bring to a boil. Check the potatoes after 2 to 3 minutes of boiling; if warm in the center, they are done. Drain thoroughly.
2. Preheat oven to 350°.
3. Rub a gratin or oven-proof baking dish with garlic and butter the dish liberally.
4. Arrange the potato slices in layers, sprinkling each layer with salt, pepper and nutmeg. There should be 2 to 3 layers.
5. Add enough heavy cream to cover. Bake the gratin for 1½ hours. The gratin is cooked when the cream is well reduced and drops of butter begin to form around the edge of the dish.

You have to love this business. Small restaurants don't make millionaires. The restaurant has to be in your heart—you have to feel for it.

My wine steward is a gentleman, not a pressure guy. He loves wine— he's been studying wine ever since he came to work here. Why, he knows more about wine than I do!

PINEAPPLE WITH RUM

Skimping on the quality of the rum in this recipe will ruin the dessert. We use a dark rum called Myers's, which has lots of flavor.

Hawaiian pineapples are far superior to those of Texas. Hawaiian pineapples seem to be flavorful and ripe all year 'round. Don't waste your time on the Texas variety.

Juice and grated rind of 3 medium limes
2 ounces dark rum
1 large Hawaiian pineapple, peeled, cored and cut into large chunks
    (work over a bowl to catch all the juice)

1. Place the pineapple chunks with reserved juices in a bowl and mix in the lime juice, rind and rum.
2. Chill for several hours in the refrigerator.
3. Serve the pineapple with its juice in wine or water goblets.

LEGAL SEA FOODS®

Dinner for Six

Stuffed Top Neck Clams

Fish Chowder

Steamed Haddock with Vegetables

Orange Sorbet Colada

Wine:

*With Stuffed Clams and Chowder—Muscadet de Sèvre
et Maine Sur Lie (Louis Metaireau) 1977
With Steamed Haddock—Johannisberg Riesling
(Ste. Michelle) 1978*

The Berkowitz Family, Proprietors

"If it isn't fresh, it isn't legal," is the motto of New England's premier seafood house, Legal Sea Foods. For three decades Legal's owners, the Berkowitz family, have been supplying Boston with its freshest seafood. The Berkowitzes sell a staggering twenty-seven tons of ocean-fresh fish weekly. Their newest restaurant alone serves 1,500 fish dinners a day.

Cambridge fish lovers fondly remember the first Legal Sea Foods restaurant, which opened in Inman Square in 1968. The fresh fish from the adjacent fish market was fried to order and served unceremoniously on paper plates with plastic cutlery. "In the beginning, our formula was to cut down on atmosphere and ambience, to splurge on the food instead," recalls George Berkowitz. The formula worked wonders, for soon piscophiles from all over New England were waiting in block-long lines to savor the Legal seafood.

The sleek, new Legal's downtown has come a long way from the paper plates and picnic tables of the Inman Square eatery. "We also wanted a restaurant where people could dine more elegantly," says Roger Berkowitz, who runs the downtown Legal's. So when space became available in the former Terrace Room of the Park Plaza Hotel last January, the Berkowitzes leapt at the opportunity to launch their third Legal Sea Foods restaurant. Canvas hangings, brass railings and a soft blue-and-white color scheme create a maritime atmosphere at the new Legal's. The bright, multitiered dining area, suggesting the decks of a stately ship, seats 200, with room for seventy-five more in the lounge.

The Legal's system, with its rotating servers and pay-when-you-order policy, perplexes newcomers to the restaurant. "Unlike most restaurants, we refuse to hold one dish under a heat lamp until the entire order is ready," Roger Berkowitz explains. "As soon as a dish is ready, it is served by the first available waitress. To us at Legal Sea Foods, protocol is second to taste."

THE BOSTON PARK PLAZA
43 BOYLSTON STREET
BOSTON

STUFFED TOP NECK CLAMS

*Top neck clams are a little smaller than cherrystones and are more
flavorful. Do not use quahogs—clams with shells larger than 3"—
they are too tough.*

12 live top neck or cherrystone clams, well scrubbed
1 small onion, finely chopped
1 branch celery, finely chopped
½ green pepper, cored, seeded and finely chopped
2 tablespoons butter
2 tablespoons finely chopped parsley
1 cup dry white wine
¾ cup dried bread crumbs
1 tablespoon Dijon-style mustard
Salt and freshly ground black pepper
½ cup toasted, slivered almonds

1. Place clams in a saucepan with ¼" water and steam, covered, until
   shells open. Remove the clams from the shells and chop, reserving
   shell bottoms.
2. Strain and reserve the clam broth.
3. Sauté the onion, celery and green pepper in butter until soft.
   Stir in the parsley, wine, bread crumbs, mustard and chopped clams.
   Add enough of the clam broth to make a moist stuffing. Season to taste.
4. Divide the clam stuffing evenly among the reserved shells and top
   with toasted almonds. (The stuffed clams can be prepared ahead of
   time to this point.)
5. Preheat oven to 450°.
6. Bake for 15 minutes and serve at once.

*I have never understood why someone would take a very successful
recipe, one which no one has ever been able to duplicate, and give
it away to the public. These recipes retain the flavor of Legal Sea
Foods, but they have been modified from what we actually offer on
our menu.*

FISH CHOWDER

For a richer chowder, you can substitute fish stock for the water in the recipe. To make fish stock, ask your fishmonger for fish heads and fish bones and simmer the bones with vegetables and aromatic herbs. (Note: recipes for fish stock appear elsewhere in this book.)

There is no need to add flour to this fish chowder—the potatoes act as a thickener in themselves.

2 onions, finely chopped
2 leeks, white part only, finely chopped
¼ cup butter
4 potatoes, peeled and diced
Salt and freshly ground black pepper
2 cups boiling water or fish stock (see index)
1 pound mixed cod and flounder
3 cups light cream
½ cup grated Swiss cheese

1. Sauté the onions and leeks in butter until soft. Add the potatoes, salt, pepper and water or fish stock and bring to a boil.
2. Layer the fish on top of the vegetables, reduce heat and simmer the chowder, covered, for 30 minutes.
3. Add the light cream and warm, but do not boil. Correct the seasoning.
4. To serve, ladle the chowder into oven-proof soup bowls and sprinkle with grated cheese. Place in a very hot oven or under the broiler and cook until the cheese is melted and golden. Serve immediately.

"Fresh fish" is a misnomer at most restaurants. All it means, technically, is that the fish has not been frozen. Fish caught the first day of a ten-day fishing trip is not very fresh by our standards.

STEAMED HADDOCK WITH VEGETABLES

6 (9-ounce) pieces of filet of haddock
6 carrots, peeled and cut into ¼" x ¼" x 2" sticks
1½ pounds zucchini, thinly sliced
1½ pounds broccoli, coarse stems discarded, broken into florets
1 pound straw or regular mushrooms, washed and quartered
3 tablespoons butter
12 thin slices tomato
1½ pounds mild Cheddar cheese (or cheese of your choice), grated

1. Overlap 2 sheets of 12" x 16" aluminum foil on a work surface to form a 12" x 19" rectangle. Place a piece of haddock in the center. Arrange one-sixth of the carrots, zucchini, broccoli and mushrooms in small piles around the fish, alternating colors. Dot the fish and vegetables with butter. Place 2 slices of tomato on top of the fish and sprinkle a handful of cheese on top. Fold the flaps of foil over the fish and seal the top and edges to form a tent around the filling. Make 5 more fish-vegetable tents following the procedure described above.
2. Preheat oven to 450°.
3. Bake fish bundles for 35 to 40 minutes. Open 1 bundle to make sure the fish is cooked—it should pull apart easily in moist flakes. For serving, slash the foil along the bottom and slide fish and vegetables onto warm dinner plates.

Truly fresh fish will not have a fishy smell. When you run your finger along a filet of fresh fish, nothing should come off.

When fish is cooked, its translucent grey color will turn white. The flesh should come apart in moist flakes.

ORANGE SORBET COLADA

½ cup plus 2 tablespoons white rum
½ cup plus 2 tablespoons triple sec
3 tablespoons grenadine
1½ cups fresh orange juice
1 (12-ounce) can piña colada mix
3 cups crushed ice
1 orange, thinly sliced

Place all ingredients except orange slices in a blender and churn for 45 seconds or until the colada is of soft serving consistency. (You may need to do it in 2 batches for this quantity.) Pour into chilled 12-ounce wine glasses and garnish with orange slices for serving.

L'espalier

Dinner for Six

Bay Scallops à la Nage

Lamb Noisettes with Onion and Mint

Bing Cherry Clafoutis

Wine:

With Lamb—Château Malartic-Lagravière Graves 1971
With Scallops—Vouvray Sec (Clos du Bourg) 1974

Moncef Meddeb, Proprietor and Chef
Dona Doll, Proprietor

You don't have to tell Moncef Meddeb about the rigors and privations of the restaurant trade. Six days a week the indefatigable owner of L'Espalier on Boylston Street spends fifteen hours on his feet, hand-picking the day's produce, butchering his own meats, simmering his stocks and sauces, cooking each and every dinner to order and tasting it before it goes out to the dining room. "I wonder if I have all my sanity, sometimes," he muses, "but then there are the high moments, when my cooking attains a little tiny piece of Truth and that's what keeps me going."

Truth is a pretty high-minded ideal for the restaurant business, but then L'Espalier is no commonplace restaurant. Guests ride a private elevator to the spacious second-floor dining room. The contemporary furnishings make L'Espalier both an elegant and a comfortable place to dine. L'Espalier's namesake—a pear tree trimmed and trained to grow in perfect symmetry—serves as an apt symbol for the restaurant's cuisine: the transformation of nature's finest ingredients into something considerably more sophisticated and refined.

A Tunisian by birth, Moncef Meddeb grew up outside of Paris, where his parents raised vegetables, fruit trees and rabbits. His cooking reflects his dual heritage in his fondness for the bold flavors of North Africa and his devotion to the classicism of France. Two years ago Moncef met Dona Doll, who now runs L'Espalier's dining room. Unable to find that fantasied hole-in-the-wall restaurant in Cambridge and undaunted by the haughty reputation of their Boylston Street predecessors, the pair bravely purchased the former Dodin Bouffant—reputed to have been one of the best and most pretentious establishments in the city— in which to open their first restaurant.

L'Espalier's offerings—a felicitous blend of nouvelle and classical French cuisine—vary daily. "Of course we cause ourselves extra hardship by changing the menu so often," Moncef concedes. "But the reality of the fish and produce out there changes daily, too." With four kitchen hands to a limited forty seats in the dining room, L'Espalier has one of the highest chef-to-client ratios in Boston. "Without the extra hands, we just couldn't serve the kind of food we believe in," Moncef says.

384 BOYLSTON STREET
BOSTON

BAY SCALLOPS A LA NAGE

Nager *is the French word for* "*swim.*" *The scallops* à la nage *in this recipe do their swimming in a spicy broth.*

18 snow pea pods
⅔ cup freshly shucked sweet peas
2 large tomatoes
1 teaspoon freshly grated orange peel
1 quart boiling water
Court Bouillon
1½ pounds Bay, Cape or small sea scallops, small half-moon
   muscle removed from the sides
½ teaspoon sherry vinegar
5⅓ tablespoons unsalted butter
Salt and freshly ground Szechuan peppercorns

1. Plunge the snow peas into boiling, salted water for 2
   minutes. Remove with slotted spoon, rinse under cold water,
   drain and set aside. Plunge sweet peas into same boiling, salted
   water, drain and set aside.
2. To peel and seed the tomatoes, slash an "x" on the bottom of
   each tomato, plunge into boiling water for 10 seconds, rinse under
   cold water and slip off the skins. Cut tomatoes in half widthwise
   and wring out the seeds and pulp with the palm of your hand.
   Chop the tomatoes coarsely and set aside.
3. Place the orange peel in a strainer and pour 1 quart of boiling
   water over it.
4. Preheat oven to 150°.
5. Strain the **Court Bouillon**, reserving the vegetables, and bring to a
   boil. Add the scallops and cook for 2 minutes. Remove the scallops
   with a slotted spoon and divide evenly among 6 serving bowls. Keep
   warm in oven.
6. Reduce the **Court Bouillon** at a rapid boil for 2 minutes and add
   the sherry vinegar. Whisk in the butter rapidly, followed by the
   snow peas, fresh peas, tomatoes, orange peel and a few of the
   vegetables reserved from the strained **Court Bouillon**.
7. Remove from heat and season to taste. Ladle the nage over the
   scallops and serve at once.

Court Bouillon

This makes five and one-half cups.

6 cups water
2 carrots, peeled and thinly sliced
1 leek, white part only, washed and thinly sliced
8 small white onions, peeled and thinly sliced
2 shallots, peeled and thinly sliced
Following ingredients tied up in a cheesecloth:
    2 unpeeled cloves garlic
    2 strips lemon peel
    1 clove
    1 bay leaf
    Pinch of thyme
    Sprig of parsley
    ½ teaspoon fennel seeds
1 cup dry white wine

1. Combine all ingredients except the wine in a large pot and simmer for 30 minutes.
2. Add the wine, bring the broth just to a boil and remove from heat. Discard the cheesecloth spice bag and cool.

Court Bouillon means "brief broth," literally, referring to the fact that water has been used to prepare this poaching liquid, instead of the customary, long-simmered fish stock.

A cook can never be too alert in a restaurant kitchen.

LAMB NOISETTES WITH ONION AND MINT

To reinforce the lamb flavor, you can add a touch of demiglace—made by simmering roast lamb bones in veal stock to cover and cooking until only a few tablespoons of stock remain.

2 large onions, peeled and quartered
1 quart lamb stock
¼ cup heavy cream
Salt, pepper, freshly grated nutmeg
1 tablespoon olive oil
½ cup unsalted butter
6 (6-ounce) lamb noisettes (thick steaks cut from the loin or
   tenderloin)
2 shallots, minced
2 tablespoons sherry wine vinegar
2 tablespoons meat glaze (optional)
12 fresh mint leaves
Fresh Sweet Peas

1. Simmer the onions in lamb stock until very, very soft. Remove onions with a slotted spoon and purée in a food processor or blender. Set aside the onion-flavored stock. Transfer the onion purée to a heavy saucepan and simmer for a few minutes to evaporate most of the moisture. Add the heavy cream and simmer for a few more minutes. Season with salt, pepper and nutmeg. Set aside and keep warm.
2. Preheat oven to 450°.
3. Heat the olive oil with 2 tablespoons butter in a sauté pan and sear the lamb noisettes on all sides. Finish cooking the lamb on a hot broiling pan in the oven for 10 to 12 minutes for medium rare or to taste. When the lamb is cooked as desired, remove it from the oven and let it rest for 2 minutes. Meanwhile, discard all but 1 teaspoon fat in the sauté pan and add the shallots. Cook the shallots for 30 seconds or until lightly browned. Deglaze the pan with the sherry vinegar and simmer until most of the liquid has evaporated. Add the stock and continue simmering until 1 cup liquid remains. Whisk in the meat glaze, if using, and correct the seasoning. Set aside and keep warm.
4. Warm 6 large dinner plates. Mince the mint leaves and stir them into the onion purée. Whisk the remaining butter into the hot sauce in little pieces.
5. Thinly slice the lamb noisettes and fan out the pieces at the top of each plate. Spoon the onion purée onto the center of each plate and sprinkle with the **Fresh Sweet Peas**. Ladle the sauce around the edge of each plate, not over the lamb or onion, and serve the noisettes at once.

Fresh Sweet Peas

1½ cups freshly shucked sweet peas
1 quart boiling, salted water
¼ cup unsalted butter
Salt and pepper

Plunge peas into boiling, salted water and cook for 3 minutes. Rinse
peas under cold running water to fix the color and drain. Just prior
to serving, melt the butter in a sauté pan and cook peas for 2 to 3 more
minutes or until tender. Season with salt and pepper and serve.

*There is something very discouraging about the fine food aspect of
American restaurants. We all work at a disadvantage—we have miniscule
staffs. You just can't replace the thirty-six skilled hands you find in a
three-star French restaurant with the eight untrained hands we have here.*

BING CHERRY CLAFOUTIS

3 cups fresh Bing or black cherries, pitted and stems removed
½ cup kirschwasser
¾ cup heavy cream
2 whole eggs
6 tablespoons sugar
Orange blossom water
1   9" pie shell made with **Pâte Royale**

1. Soak the cherries in the kirschwasser for 1 hour.
2. Preheat oven to 400°.
3. Blend the cream, eggs and sugar together, adding a few drops
   orange blossom water for flavor.
4. Drain the cherries and arrange in a pre-baked pie shell. Pour the
   egg mixture over the cherries and bake in preheated oven for 20
   minutes or until an inserted skewer comes out clean. Serve either
   warm or cold.

Note: Orange blossom water—a fragrant, perfumy flavoring—is
available in most Middle Eastern or Armenian markets.

Pâte Royale

1 cup unsalted butter
2 cups all-purpose white flour
1 teaspoon salt
1½ teaspoons sugar
2 egg yolks
3 tablespoons heavy cream

1. Cut the butter finely into the flour and turn out onto a flat work surface. Make a well in the butter-flour mixture and place the remaining ingredients in the center. Mix the liquid ingredients with the fingertips, gradually incorporating the flour, and knead with the heel of the palm to obtain a smooth dough. Work the dough as little as possible. Chill dough for at least 30 minutes before rolling it out.
2. Preheat oven to 375°.
3. Tap the dough with a rolling pin to soften it and roll dough out to a ³/₈" thickness. Line a 9" pie pan with the dough and chill for 10 minutes. (You will probably have a little dough left over—use it to make little cookies.)
4. Prick the bottom of the pie shell with a fork and line with a sheet of parchment paper or tinfoil. Fill the pie shell with rice. (This helps the dough hold its shape while baking.)
5. Bake the lined tart shell in preheated oven for 20 minutes. Remove the rice and paper and continue baking for 5 to 7 minutes to dry out the bottom of the crust.

If you're in the restaurant business to make money—with a fine restaurant, at least—you probably ought to try another profession . . . . You have to have a generous nature in your cooking. I am both the owner and the chef of L'Espalier. More often than not, it's the chef who dictates the expenditures.

I tend to be a lot less happy with my cooking than my customers are.

Cooking is a process of association. When I open a cookbook, I am looking for novel ways to combine ingredients. Nouvelle cuisine hasn't really invented anything—it has just reshuffled the cards.

LOCKE-OBER CAFE

EST.-1875

WINTER PLACE

Dinner for Four

Oysters à la Gino

Lobster Stew

Breast of Chicken Sauté à la Richmond

Belgian Endive Salad with House Dressing

Indian Pudding

Wine:

*With Oysters—Johannisberg Riesling
(Rutherford Hill) 1978
With Chicken—Chardonnay (San Martin) 1978
With Pudding—Lake Country Muscat Canelli
(Fetzer) 1978*

Frank Curro, General Manager

Boston has changed a lot since 1875 when Louis Ober opened his Restaurant Parisien at 4 Winter Place. However, at his legacy—the Locke-Ober Café—time has stood still. Guests still dine amid the splendor of the Gay '90s—the gold-leaf wallpaper and hand-carved Dominican mahogany woodwork; the gleaming silver steam tables and bronze *Gloria Victis*, a statue which doubles as a hat rack; the rose nude portrait of Mademoiselle Yvonne, to whom generations of bons vivants have raised toasts. It is true that ten years ago "ladies" dared to cross the threshold of Locke-Ober's hallowed Men's Bar on the ground floor. Despite the architectural and social upheavals which have swept the rest of Boston, though, the Locke-Ober Café has remained much as it was when it opened over a century ago.

It is often said that fine food and vintage wine are a heaven-made marriage. The initial union of Frank Locke's Wine Rooms and Louis Ober's Restaurant Parisien, however, was anything but felicitous. Frank Locke, a retired sea captain, spurned the fancy French fare of his Winter Place neighbor and set up shop next door to Ober's place in 1891, purveying hard liquor, Maine lobster and solid steak and potatoes. In time the public came to prefer Locke's for drinking, but Ober's for dining, and would file from one establishment to the other through a narrow door which joined them.

The competition ended in 1894, when a liquor company purchased both restaurants. The key to the door which separated them was ceremoniously tossed into the Boston Harbor and the modern Locke-Ober's was born. A Frenchman, Emile Camus, who reigned over 4 Winter Place for the next forty-five years, undertook the task of uniting the restaurants. To this day, Locke-Ober's bill of fare combines the extravagance of Ober's continental cuisine with the hardy Yankee cooking of the Maine sea captain, Locke.

"On any given day we have at least sixty-five items to choose from," boasts Locke-Ober's current general manager, Frank Curro. "The menu changes daily according to what's in season and every dish is cooked to order." Curro began his career at Locke-Ober's as a busboy forty years ago and has risen through the ranks to become head man at the ten-room, 300-seat restaurant. "I accepted the job because I love my help and my customers," he says. "I want this place to remain just as it was in the old days—a fine place where our clients were not just customers, but close friends."

4 WINTER PLACE
BOSTON

OYSTERS A LA GINO

*Thirty years ago Chef Gino Bertolaccini, experimenting with Oysters
Rockefeller, invented the following dish.*

2 cloves garlic, peeled
12 lean strips bacon
2 cups fresh crab meat
4 teaspoons paprika
1¼ cups **Cream Sauce**
¼ cup Madeira wine
Salt and freshly ground black pepper
1½ cups fresh bread crumbs
¼ cup olive oil
Rock salt
24 large oysters, freshly opened
Lemon wedges

1. Preheat oven to 375°.
2. Mince 1 clove garlic with 4 strips bacon and fry until the bacon
   is crisp. Pour off fat. Blend the bacon-garlic mixture with the crab
   meat and 2 teaspoons paprika. Fold in **Cream Sauce**, wine, salt and
   pepper. Bring to a quick boil, pour into a shallow pan and cool.
3. Mince the remaining garlic and mix with bread crumbs, remaining
   paprika and olive oil.
4. Cover 4 oven-proof plates with a ¼" layer of rock salt and place
   6 large oysters on the half shell on each plate. Spoon a generous
   mound of the crab meat mixture on each oyster, then sprinkle on
   a layer of bread crumbs.
5. Cut remaining bacon strips in thirds. Top each oyster with a curled
   piece of raw bacon.
6. Bake in preheated oven for 15 minutes or until the bacon is crisp
   and the crumb topping is brown. Serve at once with lemon wedges.

Cream Sauce

This makes about three cups. Use remainder for the chicken.

6 tablespoons butter
6 tablespoons flour
1½ cups milk
1½ cups light cream
Pinch of salt

1. Melt butter over a double boiler, stir in flour and let cook for
   10 minutes.
2. Scald milk and cream in a separate pan and whisk gradually into
   the butter-flour mixture.
3. Add salt and cook slowly for 45 minutes, stirring from time to time.

LOBSTER STEW

*When John F. Kennedy lunched at Locke-Ober's, he would invariably
order the Lobster Stew. "The broth is for me," he would say and give
his waiter the lobster meat.*

1½ pounds cooked lobster meat, diced
½ cup unsalted butter
Tomalley from the lobster (optional)
1 teaspoon paprika
2 cups light cream
2 cups milk
Salt and freshly ground black pepper

1. Gently sauté the lobster in 6 tablespoons butter in a 2-quart
   saucepan for 3 to 4 minutes or until the meat is firm. Add the
   tomalley and paprika and sauté briefly.
2. Pour in the cream and milk and heat thoroughly, but do not let
   boil. Season to taste and ladle into a soup tureen.
3. Float the remaining butter on top and serve immediately with
   pilot crackers.

Note: Some people like to add Tabasco or Worcestershire sauce, but
this should be left to the diner's discretion.

BREAST OF CHICKEN SAUTE A LA RICHMOND

This dish would be really nice with a smoked ham, like Smithfield ham. If you use smoked ham, it should be very thinly sliced.

6 tablespoons butter
4 boned chicken breasts
12 medium-sized mushroom caps
¾ cup sherry
¾ cup light cream
4 slices of cooked ham (about ¼" thick), cut to the size of a piece
    of toast
Cream Sauce (remainder from oysters)
Salt and pepper to taste
4 slices toasted white bread, trimmed of crusts

1. Preheat oven to 350°.
2. Melt half the butter in a large sauté pan and add the chicken, skin
    side down. Sauté for 5 minutes or until golden brown. Turn the
    breasts and add the mushroom caps. Cook for 5 minutes, pour off fat
    and add half the sherry, half the cream, the ham, the **Cream Sauce**
    and the seasonings. Cover and bake for 30 minutes.
3. Place a piece of toast in each of 4 shirred egg dishes or individual au
    gratin dishes. Remove ham, chicken and mushrooms from sauce;
    arrange ham slices on top of toast, chicken breasts on top of ham
    and divide the mushroom caps evenly among the dishes. Whisk the
    remaining sherry, cream and butter into the sauce left in the pan and
    simmer for 3 minutes. Strain sauce over chicken.
4. Cover each dish with a glass bell *(sous cloche)* and place in a hot
    oven until the condensation under the glass clears. If you do not
    have glass bells, omit this step and serve at once.

Locke-Ober's is an institution, you see. We don't try to compete with other restaurants. We try to stay with the dishes which made Locke-Ober's great to begin with. If someone wants something that's not on our menu and we have the ingredients, we'll be glad to make it. We want people to really feel at home at Locke-Ober's.

BELGIAN ENDIVE SALAD WITH HOUSE DRESSING

4 large leaves Boston lettuce
4 stalks Belgian endive, cut into large strips
4 large pieces of canned hearts of palm, quartered lengthwise
4 small cooked beets, diced
1 cup **House Dressing**

1. Cover 4 chilled salad plates with lettuce leaves.
2. Place a bundle of endive in the center of each plate. Garnish
   with hearts of palm pieces and beets.
3. Spoon the **House Dressing** over the salad for serving.

House Dressing

$2/3$ teaspoon salt
¼ teaspoon paprika
$1/3$ teaspoon dry mustard
$1/3$ teaspoon white pepper
Juice of ½ lemon
4 tablespoons cider vinegar
1 clove garlic, crushed
¾ cup olive oil
1 tablespoon finely chopped pimiento
1 tablespoon chopped fresh green pepper
1½ teaspoons chopped parsley
1½ teaspoons chopped scallions

Combine all of the ingredients in a large jar and shake to mix thoroughly.

Note: The dressing must be shaken directly before pouring over
the salad.

INDIAN PUDDING

This is one of our most famous dishes. It should be served with a scoop of vanilla ice cream.

¼ cup corn meal
2 cups cold milk
2 cups scalded milk
½ cup molasses
1 teaspoon salt
¼ cup sugar
½ teaspoon cinnamon
½ teaspoon ginger
4 tablespoons butter
2 tablespoons white rum

1. Preheat oven to 250°.
2. Mix the corn meal with enough cold milk to pour easily. Stir until smooth. Slowly add the scalded milk and cook over a double boiler for 20 minutes or until the mixture thickens.
3. Add the molasses, salt, sugar, cinnamon, ginger and butter and pour into a buttered pudding dish. Pour the remaining cold milk and rum over the pudding.
4. Set the dish in a pan of hot water and bake in preheated oven for 3 hours. Let stand ½ hour before serving.

A good chef is someone who works his way up through the ranks. Most of our employees have worked their way up. Even our chef came here as a dishwasher. A good chef is someone who, no matter how much he knows, is always willing to listen, to try something a new way. He is someone who is proud of his product, who is willing to please, who can get along with other people.

maison robert

Dinner for Four

Potage Santé
(Sorrel Soup)

Terrine de Poireaux au Coulis de Tomates
(Terrine of Leeks with a Fresh Tomato Sauce)

Estouffade de Lotte au Muscadet
(Monkfish Cooked in Muscadet Wine)

Céleris Braises
(Braised Celery)

Tarte Tatin
(Upside-Down Apple Pie)

Wine:

With Meal—Muscadet sur Lie Cuvée de Prestige
(L. Metaireau) 1977-78
With Tarte Tatin—Château Roumieu-Lacoste 1975

Ann and Lucien Robert, Proprietors
Jacques Morel and Pierre Jamet, Chefs

"Opening another restaurant was the last thing we had in mind," recall Ann and Lucien Robert, proprietors of the prestigious Maison Robert. But when space became available in the freshly renovated Old City Hall in 1972, the pair could not resist the stately, historic setting for a new dining establishment. Built in 1865, Old City Hall remains one of the finest examples of French Second Empire architecture in North America—in the Roberts' minds the perfect foil for Lucien's classical French cuisine.

Maison Robert is actually two restaurants. The elegant Bonhomme Richard offers formal French dining amid the high ceilings, oak paneling and serene view of King's Chapel of the former City Treasurer's office. The tastefully appointed Ben's Café in the old City Vault downstairs may be less formal, though no less elegant. The two restaurants, private dining rooms and outdoor terrace combined seat 300.

Both Bonhomme Richard and Ben's Café—named for Benjamin Franklin, whose statue graces Maison Robert's portals—serve impeccably prepared classical French cuisine. "Our chefs are free to experiment, but not on the customers," says Lucien Robert. "Every dish is tasted by my wife, my staff and me before we consider putting it on the menu." A full-time kitchen staff of twenty-five, a quarter of which are French, help Monsieur Robert uphold the quality and authenticity of his fare.

The son of farmers, Lucien Robert was born in Normandy and trained at some of the top restaurants in Paris, including Prunier and the Pavillon D'Armenomville, before coming to the United States in 1951. A year-long visit became a life-long sojourn when the young chef met his future wife Ann, a historian in Madison, Wisconsin. Drawn by the rich cultural heritage of the Bay State, they settled in Boston in 1953. Maison Robert is Lucien's third French restaurant in the city and the crowning achievement of a busy, ambitious career.

45 SCHOOL STREET
BOSTON

POTAGE SANTE

We only put Potage Santé on our menu when we have enough fresh sorrel in our garden to make it. We always serve salmon with fresh sorrel in the summertime.

2 large leeks, white part only, sliced lengthwise and thoroughly washed
4 tablespoons butter
4 medium potatoes, peeled and quartered
1 quart chicken consommé
½ pound fresh sorrel leaves
2 egg yolks
1 cup heavy cream
Salt and pepper

1. Chop the leeks and lightly sauté in 2 tablespoons butter. Add the potatoes and consommé and boil rapidly for 10 minutes or until potatoes are cooked.
2. Transfer potatoes and leeks to a blender or food processor and purée. Recombine the purée with broth.
3. Wash the sorrel and remove stems. Sauté for 2 to 3 minutes in remaining butter. Finely chop the cooked sorrel and add it to the soup.
4. Heat the soup to a simmer and mix the yolks with the cream. Little by little, whisk 1 cup of the soup into the yolk-cream mixture, then stir this back into the soup.
5. Gently warm the soup to cook the egg yolks and thicken the soup—do not let boil or the soup will curdle. Season to taste. Serve with fresh butter-fried croutons.

Like most dreams in life, mine has been difficult to obtain. To produce a perfect meal or perfect service . . . it rarely happens. The restaurant business is very challenging and every day the challenge begins anew.

As a fellow restaurateur in town here says, "I'm just as good as the last meal I cooked." It's a marvelous and humble way to express the truth of the restaurant business. . . . Our long-term goals for the restaurant are very simple: always to be better, and to have fun trying.

TERRINE DE POIREAUX AU COULIS DE TOMATES

Consistency is the most important ingredient for running a restaurant successfully. If you are consistent, your clients will never be disappointed.

This recipe will serve eight to ten people.

20 leeks, white part only, sliced to the root lengthwise
    and thoroughly washed
1 quart good beef consommé
2 envelopes gelatin, softened over ½ cup water
Salt and pepper
Coulis de Tomates

1. Tie the leeks into bundles and cook in boiling, salted water until tender. Refresh under cold running water and drain well.
2. Heat consommé until hot.
3. Melt the softened gelatin over a pan of boiling water and stir it into the hot consommé. Season to taste.
4. Cool the consommé until it is thick and oily and on the verge of setting. Dip each individual leek in the consommé and place in a 1½-quart terrine mold or loaf pan. When all the leeks are attractively arranged in the mold, pour the remaining consommé over them. Refrigerate overnight.
5. To serve, cut into ½" slices with a sharp knife. Serve the **Coulis de Tomates** on the side.

Coulis de Tomates

3 large ripe tomatoes
¼ cup good delicate red wine vinegar
¼ cup good virgin olive oil
¼ cup chopped parsley
Salt and plenty of freshly ground black pepper

1. To peel the tomatoes, cut a small "x" on the bottoms, plunge into boiling water for 10 seconds, rinse under cold water and slip off skins.
2. Halve the tomatoes widthwise and wring out the seeds and pulp with the palm of your hand.
3. Chop the tomatoes very finely and whisk in the remaining ingredients. Correct the seasoning before serving.

ESTOUFFADE DE LOTTE AU MUSCADET

We were the first restaurant in Boston to serve lotte—*monkfish.
In this country it's considered a trash fish, though in France it's
deemed a delicacy. So we would have our monkfish specially flown
in from France. Eventually we learned that American fishermen
were selling the monkfish they caught here to the French, so the
lotte which appeared on our menu had crossed the Atlantic twice!*

2 shallots, minced
6 tablespoons butter
1 leek, white part only, thinly sliced
1 carrot, peeled and finely diced
1½ pounds trimmed monkfish, cut into 1" cubes
2 cups Muscadet wine
¾ cup whipping cream
1 cup peeled seedless white grapes (optional)

1. Gently sauté shallots in 3 tablespoons butter. Stir in the chopped
   leek and carrot and continue sautéing until the vegetables are soft,
   but not browned.
2. Add the monkfish and gently sauté over medium heat for 3
   minutes, shaking the pan to thoroughly mix the fish with the
   vegetables.
3. Pour in the wine and bring almost to a boil. Remove pan from heat,
   cover and allow the fish to poach in the hot broth for 6 to 7 minutes.
4. Remove the fish and vegetables from the poaching liquid with a
   slotted spoon and transfer to a warm platter. Bring the broth to a
   boil and cook until only 3 to 4 tablespoons liquid remain.
5. Remove pan from heat and whisk in the remaining butter and whipping
   cream. Warm this sauce over a low heat, but do not let boil or it will
   curdle.
6. Add the peeled grapes to the sauce to warm, then pour the sauce over
   the monkfish and vegetables. Serve at once.

Note: Monkfish—sometimes called goosefish or angler—can be found
at gourmet seafood shops and humble ethnic fishmongers. Be sure to
trim away the wet, purplish membrane before using.

*Keeping ninety employees happy is one of my major tasks—a
restaurant is only as good as its staff.*

CELERIS BRAISES

2 bunches celery
½ cup unsalted butter
½ clove garlic, minced
½ small onion, finely chopped
1 carrot, finely diced
½ bay leaf
2 cups veal stock
Salt and pepper
¼ cup heavy cream

1. Preheat oven to 350°.
2. Remove the tops and bottoms of the celery and cut stalks in 6"
   lengths. Peel the rounded sides of the stalks with a vegetable peeler
   to remove the strings. Blanch the celery in boiling water for 3 minutes,
   rinse in cold water and drain.
3. Melt the butter in a deep pan. When it foams, add the celery pieces and
   brown on all sides. Add all remaining ingredients except the cream and
   cover. Cook over a low heat or in preheated oven until celery is very
   tender—about 40 to 50 minutes.
4. Transfer the celery to a lightly buttered, oven-proof serving dish and
   pour over it a few tablespoons of the cooking liquid, plus the heavy
   cream. Bake for 5 more minutes before serving.

*My advice to someone who wants to open a restaurant? First, prepare
yourself and thoroughly learn the business. Second, take pride in what
you do and do it well. Finally, forget about the cash register. . . . Too
many restaurateurs are too busy counting their money. If you do a
good job, the cash register will show it in the long run. Quality or profit
doesn't have to be an either/or matter. If you really apply yourself, you
can have both.*

TARTE TATIN

*The recipe for this Tarte Tatin was brought to us by a visiting chef
from Nantes. It has become one of the most popular desserts on our
menu. We make our tarts fresh every noon and evening. Our
Tarte Tatin has never seen the inside of the refrigerator.*

This recipe will serve ten.

1 cup, plus 2 tablespoons unsalted butter
1½ cups sugar
Juice of 1 lemon
20 Golden Delicious apples, peeled, cored and halved
Pâte Brisée

1. Preheat oven to 375°.
2. Smear a tarte tatin mold or 16" cast-iron frying pan with the butter
   and sprinkle with the sugar. Arrange the apple halves in the mold in
   overlapping spirals—they should be quite closely packed together—
   and sprinkle with lemon juice. Cook the apples over a medium flame
   until the sugar caramelizes and the bottoms of the apples turn a
   golden brown.
3. Remove from heat and cover the top of the pan with a circle of
   Pâte Brisée rolled to a thickness of ⅜". Bake the tart in preheated
   oven for 1 hour.
4. Remove from the oven and place a round serving platter on top. Invert
   the frying pan without delay—the tart should slide easily from the mold.

Note: Serve warm with crème fraîche or whipped cream on the side.

Pâte Brisée

1 cup, less 2 tablespoons butter
2½ cups flour
¼ cup sugar
Pinch of salt
½ cup cold water

Cut the butter into the flour with a pastry cutter. Add the sugar and
salt to the water and blend lightly with the flour-butter mixture.
Gently knead the dough into a ball. Chill for at least 2 hours before
rolling out into desired round shape.

*My first advice for making Tarte Tatin is to completely line the top
of your stove with tin foil before starting. That way, when the tart
spatters, you won't spend your whole night cleaning your stove top!*

modern gourmet boston
"la bonne bouche"
AN imaginative RESTAURANT

Dinner for Four

Salade Composé
*(Salad of Shrimp, Pears, Beets and Belgian Endive,
Served with Ginger Mayonnaise)*

Grapefruit Sorbet

Chicken en Papillote
*(Chicken with Fontina Cheese and Mushroom
Compote, Cooked in a Paper Envelope)*

Jardinière de Legumes
(Medley of Seasonal Vegetables)

Nocciolo
(Hazelnut Ice Cream with Chocolate Sauce)

Wine:

*With Salad—Mâcon-Villages (Chaderdon) 1976
With Chicken—Moulin-à-Vent (Heritiers Finaz
Devillaine) 1978*

Patrick von Hoyningen Huene, Chef

MODERN GOURMET
(LA BONNE BOUCHE)

The imperious Madeleine Kamman no longer owns the restaurant/ cooking school Modern Gourmet in Newton Centre, but the spirit of the renowned French food authority lives on at La Bonne Bouche. All the chefs are Modern Gourmet graduates, as are the current owners, who purchased the restaurant from Kamman last October. Today, as when Modern Gourmet opened six years ago, the basement dining room has much of the atmosphere of a French country inn, with exposed ceiling beams and brick walls adorned with copper cookware. As in the first days of Kamman's tenure, this fine dining establishment is open on weekends only.

This is not, however, to deny La Bonne Bouche a unique personality of its own. "I'm not trying to mimic or recreate Madeleine's food," says executive chef, Patrick von Hoyningen Huene. "I am trying to use what she has taught me, plus my own talents, to implement a style of my own." A five-year veteran of the kitchen, the twenty-four-year-old chef brings ingredients in from all over the country and makes all his stocks, vinegars and even ice creams from scratch. His menu changes monthly, featuring regional and seasonal themes.

"I like to refer to our cooking at La Bonne Bouche as modern cuisine," says von Hoyningen Huene. "We're not really classical, though we use classical French and Italian cooking techniques. The term nouvelle cuisine doesn't really apply to us because we live in America, not France. We've been trained by a French chef to work with the best ingredients available in this country; we use time-honored techniques to come up with something which tastes great to twentieth-century palates."

Such pains have paid off in the past, fetching Modern Gourmet awards from *Holiday* magazine, the *Mobil Guide* and numerous local papers. The new staff at La Bonne Bouche stands eager to continue the fine tradition.

81 R UNION STREET
NEWTON CENTRE

The recipes on the following pages were provided by Linda Marino, the former chef of La Bonne Bouche, who has since become part of the teaching staff of the Modern Gourmet cooking school.

SALADE COMPOSE

We always have a Salade Composé on our menu. This one combines shrimp, pears, beets, endives and ginger.

16 medium shrimp, in shells
1 bunch beets
4 ripe Anjou pears
4 Belgian endives
Mustard Vinaigrette
1 head Boston lettuce, washed
Ginger Mayonnaise
Salt and pepper

1. Preheat oven to 350°.
2. Stir-fry the shrimp in hot oil until they turn pink. Cool shrimp, peel and devein.
3. Peel the beets and bake in preheated oven for 30 minutes or until a skewer or paring knife penetrates them easily. Cool beets and thinly slice across the grain.
4. Peel the pears and cut into sixths. Break up the endives. Toss each of the ingredients separately, the beets last, in enough **Mustard Vinaigrette** to moisten.
5. Line 4 chilled plates with lettuce leaves, leaving the edge of the plate showing. Arrange the shrimp, beets, pears and endives on the lettuce in a symmetrical pattern, with a space in the center for the **Ginger Mayonnaise.**
6. Spoon mayonnaise into the center of each plate and serve.

Mustard Vinaigrette

⅓ cup wine vinegar or lemon juice
1 tablespoon extra-strong Dijon-style mustard
1½ teaspoons salt
½ cup olive oil
½ cup corn oil
25 twists freshly ground pepper

Place all of the ingredients in the blender and whirl at high speed to obtain a thick emulsion.

There's no rule of thumb on making vinaigrette sauce. It's mostly a matter of taste. If you must follow guidelines, I generally use one part acid to three parts oil. But you have to taste a vinaigrette sauce a hundred times to get it right.

Ginger Mayonnaise

1 whole egg
1 egg yolk
1 teaspoon salt
2 teaspoons Dijon-style mustard
1½ cups corn oil
Juice of ½ lemon (approximately)
2 teaspoons chopped ginger root
Salt and white pepper

1. Place whole egg, egg yolk, salt and mustard in a heavy bowl and blend to a smooth, silky consistency.
2. Whisk in the oil very slowly in a thin stream to make a thick mayonnaise.
3. Add lemon juice to taste, ginger and salt and white pepper to taste.

Note: Make sure all ingredients are at room temperature. This mayonnaise can also be made in a blender.

To prepare the ginger, peel the root with a vegetable peeler. Hold the root flat and bang the cut part of the ginger with the blunt edge of your knife. The root will disintegrate and all of the ginger pieces will fall onto your cutting board, leaving the tough strings behind.

GRAPEFRUIT SORBET

If you don't like sweet dishes, skip this recipe. You have to add a certain amount of sugar to a sorbet or it won't freeze properly.

Be choosy about your grapefruits; make sure they're fresh and juicy. You cannot tell by looking. You have to go to a dependable market and buy the best quality available. If the grapefruits are dry when you cut into them, take them back.

1 cup sugar
1 cup water
4 ripe pink grapefruits (enough to yield 2 cups juice)
Pinch of salt
1 tablespoon light rum

1. Combine the sugar and water in a saucepan and cook to the soft-ball stage—239° on a sugar thermometer. If you do not have a sugar thermometer, bring the mixture to a boil, reduce heat to a simmer and cook for exactly 5 minutes. Cool the sugar syrup and reserve.
2. Squeeze the grapefruits and strain the juice. Add the juice, salt and rum to the sugar syrup. If the grapefruits are tart, you may need to add more sugar.
3. Pour the mixture into an ice-cream machine and churn according to the instructions of your particular machine. When the mixture sets, scoop it into a cake pan and ripen the sorbet for at least 4 hours in your freezer.
4. Serve in chilled champagne glasses, sprinkling with rum to taste.

A sorbet acts as a digestif and palate cleanser before the main course.

CHICKEN EN PAPILLOTE

A papillote is a cooking envelope made from parchment paper. In this recipe, it seals in the flavor and juices of the chicken. Parchment paper is specially treated with silicon and, unlike waxed paper, it does not melt when baked. Some people substitute tin foil for parchment paper— it will work, but the results will not be as good.

There is no substitute for true Italian fontina, a cheese with a salty tang, which melts beautifully. Do not use Danish or domestic fontina— they may be cheaper, but they just don't have the right flavor.

1 pound mushrooms, washed, trimmed and thinly sliced
¼ cup unsalted butter
Salt and pepper
1 cup finely chopped parsley
2 cloves garlic, smashed and minced
2 cups heavy cream
4 sheets parchment paper
4 boned chicken breasts, trimmed of all fat, skin and tendons.
½ pound grated or thinly sliced Italian fontina cheese
Grated nutmeg

1. Gently cook the mushrooms with butter, salt and pepper in a covered sauté pan for 5 minutes. Remove cover and cook for 5 to 10 minutes to evaporate all the moisture. Reserve.
2. Make a persillade by combining the parsley and garlic. Reserve.
3. Boil the cream until reduced to 1 cup. When the mushrooms and cream are cool, combine with persillade and mix. Season with salt and pepper.
4. Preheat oven to 400°.
5. To assemble the papillotes, cut 4 (14") heart shapes from the parchment paper and butter 1 side thoroughly. Place 1 chicken breast on the right half of each paper heart and season with salt and pepper. Spread the cream-parsley-mushroom mixture evenly over the chicken breasts. Top with cheese and grated nutmeg.

6. Form the paper envelopes by folding the left half of the paper heart over the chicken. Pleat the edges together, starting at the point, making a series of small folds to hermetically seal the chicken in the paper.
7. Bake in preheated oven for exactly 10 minutes. When you remove the papillotes from the oven, they should be puffed like balloons.
8. To serve, puncture the paper and slide the chicken onto warm plates.

Some people like to serve this dish directly in the parchment envelope. I don't like to eat off paper, so I show our clients the papillotes, then transfer the contents of the bag to plates for serving.

JARDINIERE DE LEGUMES

Jardinière can be made with any seasonal vegetables.

½ pound carrots
4 celery stalks
4 zucchini
2 yellow squash
¼ cup unsalted butter
Salt and pepper
Lemon juice to taste

1. Wash the vegetables and peel the carrots and the stringy sides of the celery stalks. Thinly slice the carrots on the diagonal and cut into ⅛" slivers, called julienne. Cut the celery into 2" lengths, slice once horizontally and julienne. Box cut the zucchini by removing the outside of the vegetable in 4 slices, ¼" thick. (The square core which remains can be used in vegetable soups.) Cut each of these slices into 2" lengths and julienne. Box cut and julienne the squash in the same way.
2. Melt the butter in a shallow pan and gently sauté the vegetables together, starting with the carrots, then the celery, then the squash and finally the zucchini. Do not overcook.
3. Toss the vegetables with a little salt and pepper and lemon juice before serving.

Recipes are only guidelines to help you create your personal taste. . . . Cooking is a function of personal growth. What I cook now and what I will cook a year from now may be totally different.

NOCCIOLO

You can buy already-skinned hazelnuts, but it's not too difficult to remove the peels yourself. Roast nuts on a baking sheet in a hot oven for five minutes. When the skins begin to blister, rub the hazelnuts briskly with a dish towel to remove peels.

2 cups hazelnuts, peeled
2 cups light cream
6 egg yolks
1 cup sugar
2 teaspoons vanilla
2 cups heavy cream
Ganache Sauce

1. Grind the hazelnuts finely in a food processor. It helps to grind in short spurts, otherwise you risk reducing the nuts to a gummy paste. Place ground nuts and light cream in a saucepan, bring to a boil and remove from heat.
2. Whisk the egg yolks and sugar together in a non-aluminum bowl. Gradually whisk in the hot cream-nut mixture and transfer to a heavy-bottomed saucepan.
3. Place the mixture over a low heat for a few minutes, stirring constantly with a wooden spoon. The eggs are poached when the foam subsides, the mixture thickly coats a wooden spoon and the eggy taste disappears. Do not boil or overcook or the yolks will scramble. Strain the mixture through a fine sieve and let cool.
4. Combine the yolk mixture with vanilla and heavy cream and place in your ice-cream machine. Churn according to the instructions for your machine. When the ice cream sets, transfer it to the freezer for at least 2 hours for ripening. Serve with **Ganache Sauce.**

Ganache Sauce

3 ounces Tobler or other excellent extra bittersweet chocolate
1 tablespoon unsalted butter
¼ cup heavy cream

1. Melt the chocolate and butter over a double boiler. Stir in the cream
   to lighten.
2. Serve warm on top of the ice cream.

*A chocolate's quality goes by how much starch it contains. Tobler
contains very little, as does Lindt.*

*A good chef has to like to eat, but must enjoy food for far more than
just eating.*

9 KNOX STREET

Dinner for Six

Chinese Vegetable Soup

Quiche Lorraine

Beef Wellington

Orange Cointreau Gâteau

Wine:

With Soup and Quiche—Gewürztraminer
(Hillcrest Vineyards) 1978
With Beef—Château Vieux-Certan Pommerol 1970

Jeffrey Wayne Davies, Proprietor and Chef

For as long as he can remember, Jeffrey Wayne Davies has been a cook with a passion for the theater. His stage is a miniscule kitchen in a smart eighteenth-century townhouse-turned-restaurant. The play he performs nightly is a masterful five-course dinner. The spectators make their way down a narrow alleyway in historic Bay Village. Their destination is 9 Knox Street.

Nine Knox has been the site of a restaurant for over forty years. When Davies took charge of the place in 1970, both the establishment and the environs were in sore need of upgrading. The first step for the twenty-seven-year-old Welshman was to establish a prix-fixe menu featuring soups and vegetables that change daily, plus a Beef Wellington that was soon reputed to be the best in Boston. The neighborhood derelicts and strip joints gradually gave way to tree-lined streets with brick sidewalks and gas streetlights, as Bay Village became a fashionable place to live.

Davies brings twenty years cooking experience to his current creations. With no small pride, the exuberant Welshman explains that he passed his "City and Guilds" in South Wales before coming to the United States fifteen years ago. A specialist in cake decoration, Davies has exhibited his pastry creations before American presidents, the New England Culinary Show and even the Culinary Olympics in West Germany. During his sojourn in the United States, Davies has found the time to teach for the Boston Center of Adult Education and act in the plays of his favorite composers, Gilbert and Sullivan, in addition to opening three restaurants in Boston and one in New York.

Dining at 9 Knox Street is an experience in style and atmosphere. The browns and whites of the dining area, the sturdy bronze cutlery and pewter flatware lend 9 Knox an air of country elegance. The unique townhouse setting, with seats for a mere thirty, makes 9 Knox a locale of unsurpassed intimacy and calm. "What I really hope to achieve with my restaurant is an extension of my own dining room," explains Davies, who lives in the apartment over 9 Knox. "I would like my guests to feel as comfortable as if they were sitting around my own dinner table."

9 KNOX STREET
BOSTON

CHINESE VEGETABLE SOUP

There is nothing difficult about this soup, provided you live near a Chinese market.

1 small chicken, complete with neck, liver and giblets
1 whole carrot, quartered
1 onion, peeled and quartered
1 stalk celery
1 clove garlic, peeled
1 sprig cilantro (optional)
¼ teaspoon freshly grated ginger root
1 tablespoon rice wine vinegar
1 gallon water
Pepper and very small pinch of salt
2 ounces snow peas or sugar snaps
1 cup mung bean sprouts
2 stalks bok choy, sliced into ¼" strips
½ cup canned water chestnuts, drained and sliced
1 small bunch broccoli, tough stems discarded, tops broken into florets
2 scallions, chopped
Splash of sesame oil

1. Place chicken, carrot, onion, celery, garlic, cilantro, ginger and vinegar with water in a large pot and simmer for 45 minutes or until the chicken is cooked, skimming the broth from time to time to remove any fat or foam. Remove chicken and cool.
2. Boil the broth until only 1½ quarts remain.
3. Strain broth and degrease with strips of paper towel. Season with additional salt and pepper to taste.
4. Poach the Chinese vegetables in the seasoned broth for 3 to 5 minutes or until tender crisp, starting with the broccoli and bok choy which take the longest to cook.
5. While the vegetables are cooking, remove the breast meat from the chicken, slice into strips and add to the soup. (Use the leftover bird for tomorrow's chicken salad.)
6. Garnish soup with chopped scallions and add a splash of sesame oil for extra flavor before serving.

How do I come up with these dishes? I put unusual ingredient combinations together and see how they taste. If I like the result, I serve it; if I don't, I try again.

QUICHE LORRAINE

*A quiche should be like a bacon-flavored custard—very moist,
very creamy. The worst thing you can do to quiche is to overcook it.*

This recipe serves 8.

Short Pastry Dough
8 slices cooked bacon, crumbled
4 slices cooked ham (about ¼ pound), diced
½ cup grated Cheddar cheese
¼ cup grated Parmesan cheese
5 eggs, lightly beaten
1 clove garlic, crushed
3 cups light cream
Salt and pepper
Freshly grated nutmeg

1. Preheat oven to 350°.
2. Line an 8" x 1½" quiche pan with **Short Pastry Dough** and
   sprinkle the bacon, ham, Cheddar and Parmesan on the bottom.
3. Beat the eggs with the garlic, light cream and seasonings and pour
   into the shell.
4. Bake the quiche on the bottom rack of preheated oven for
   30 to 40 minutes or until the custard has set. (Check for doneness
   after 30 minutes—an inserted skewer should come out clean.)
   Allow quiche to cool slightly before serving.

Short Pastry Dough

2 cups unbleached white flour
Pinch of salt
½ cup Crisco
½ cup ice water

1. Sift the flour and salt into a mixing bowl and rub the Crisco through
   the flour with your fingertips to obtain a mixture with the consistency
   of bread crumbs.
2. Quickly stir in ice water to obtain a compact mass of dough.
   Do not overmix.
3. Chill for at least 30 minutes before rolling.

*I see the whole restaurant business as theater. People want to be
entertained as well as fed. God knows the restaurateur has to smile
sometimes when he doesn't feel like it.*

BEEF WELLINGTON

Wellingtons have to cook at a very high temperature so that the pastry bakes while the meat remains rare. Multiple coats of egg glaze will help the pastry brown more evenly.

6 (8-ounce) filet mignon steaks
3 ounces pâté de foie gras de Strasbourg
Salt and pepper
Puff Pastry
Water
2 eggs beaten with a pinch of salt for egg glaze

1. Trim the steaks of fat and gristle and cut a horizontal pocket in each. Stuff with pâté de foie gras and lightly season with salt and pepper.
2. Roll out the **Puff Pastry** to a thickness of ⅜'' and cut out 6 rounds large enough to completely enclose the steaks. Place a filet mignon in the center of each circle, brush the edges of the pastry with water and fold the dough over the beef to form a neat bundle. Invert onto a baking sheet.
3. Brush each Wellington with egg glaze and decorate with the leftover scraps of dough. Refrigerate for 1 hour, brushing with egg glaze 3 more times.
4. Preheat oven to 450°.
5. Brush the Wellingtons 1 final time with egg glaze and bake in oven for 15 minutes or to taste. (Fifteen minutes will give you beef which is nice and rare.) Serve immediately.

This recipe calls for pâté de foie gras, which is less expensive than pure foie gras. If you can afford to purchase the latter, by all means do so—it costs the sky, but you can really taste the difference.

Puff Pastry

4 cups unbleached white flour
1 teaspoon salt
Pinch of cream of tartar
2 tablespoons softened butter
2 cups frozen butter, cut into 1" cubes
¾ to 1 cup ice water

1. Sift the flour, salt and cream of tartar into a mixing bowl. Rub the softened butter through the flour with your fingertips to obtain a mixture with the consistency of bread crumbs.
2. Distribute the frozen butter through the mixture and stir in enough water to obtain a soft, compact mass of dough. Do not overmix. Chill for 10 minutes.
3. Lightly flour your work surface and roll out the dough to form an 18" x 15" rectangle. Fold the short ends over to meet at the center, then fold this rectangle in half. You should end up with a dough "book" with 2 "pages," each page being a double thickness of dough—4 layers in all. Cover with a damp cloth and chill for 1 hour.
4. Place dough on a floured work surface, "spine" of the dough book to your left, and roll out the dough to form another 18" x 15" rectangle. Fold again as described above, cover and chill for 1 hour. Roll, fold and chill the dough in this manner 2 more times, for a total of 4 folds and turns in all. The dough is now ready for use.

ORANGE COINTREAU GATEAU

This cake serves 12.

It is difficult to describe the "ribbon stage" to someone who is not familiar with baking. When you lift the whisk from the batter, the yolk mixture should fall in a ribbon thick enough to write a three-letter word. If the mixture is at the right consistency, the first letter will just begin to fade as you finish the third. Do not over-ribbon the yolk mixture or the cake will collapse when baked.

6 eggs, separated
¾ cup sugar
8 ounces ground almonds
Grated rind of 3 oranges

¼ cup cornstarch
1 tablespoon fine cake or cookie crumbs
2 tablespoons Cointreau
Orange Buttercream Icing
Segments from 6 oranges, rind and seeds removed

1. Preheat the oven to 350°.
2. Thoroughly butter and flour 3 (8") cake pans.
3. Ribbon the egg yolks with the sugar, that is, whisk vigorously until the mixture is smooth, creamy and tripled in volume—it should fall from a raised whisk in a thick, silky ribbon.
4. Beat the egg whites to stiff peaks.
5. Delicately fold the almonds, orange rind, cornstarch and crumbs into the yolk mixture, followed by the stiffly beaten egg whites.
6. Divide the batter between the cake pans and bake in preheated oven 15 to 18 minutes. (When cooked, the cakes will feel firm to the touch and begin to pull away from the sides of the pans; an inserted toothpick will come out clean.) Cool slightly and turn the cakes onto cake racks to cool completely.
7. Sprinkle each cake generously with Cointreau and spread with icing, reserving 1 cup icing to decorate the top. Arrange orange segments on 2 of the iced cake layers, reserving the prettiest segments for the top of the cake. Stack the cake layers. Decorate the top layer with rosettes of icing and the remaining orange segments.

Orange Buttercream Icing

2 cups unsalted butter, softened
2¼ cups confectioners' sugar
3 egg yolks
Grated rind of 3 oranges
2 tablespoons Cointreau

Whisk the butter and sugar together, gradually adding the yolks, orange peel and Cointreau. Continue beating until the mixture attains a smooth, spreadable consistency.

Nino's Place
at

Maitre' Jacques

Dinner for Four

Petite Marmite Henri IV

Noisettes d'Agneau à la Duchesse de Berry

Salade Tropicale

Soufflé Glacé au Citron

Wine:

As an Apéritif and with Dessert: Dom Pérignon
(Moët et Chandon) 1971
With Lamb—Châteauneuf-du-Pape 1970

Nino Todesco, Proprietor
Vincent Donato, Chef

If anyone knows about hospitality in Boston, it is Nino Todesco. The dapper owner of Nino's Place at Maître Jacques has made his living playing the perfect host for forty years. Todesco remembers waiting on the late Shah and Princess Farah when they honeymooned at the luxurious Casino Hotel in Venice. Recent guests to his own restaurant include Zsa Zsa Gabor, Jack Lemmon and the Queen of Thailand.

Born near Venice, Todesco entered the food trade at age fifteen and worked at top hotels in Rome, Milan and Paris, before venturing to North America in 1966. For many years Todesco served as the maître d' at Boston's swank Ritz-Carlton. At fifty-three, he decided to put his long experience to work for himself so he purchased a bastion of Boston hostelry, Maître Jacques. The stylish Charles River Place eating establishment fulfills Todesco's lifelong ambition to have his own restaurant.

"In the long run I plan to drop the name Maître Jacques and just call the restaurant Nino's Place," says Todesco. As the map on the cover of Todesco's menu suggests, Nino's Place specializes in the cooking of France, Germany, Switzerland and Northern Italy. "Our service is French," explains Todesco, who purchased the ninety-five-seat restaurant two years ago from the owners of Maison Robert.

Vincent Donato, Maître Jacques's chef, brings experience from three continents to his culinary handiwork in the Nino's Place kitchen. Born in Algeria, Vincent trained in Paris and came to the United States in 1958. He apprenticed with Réné Verdun, chef to President Kennedy, and worked eight years at the posh New York restaurants La Caravelle and Le Pavillon. More recently, Vincent cooked at a popular New England nightclub before he accepted the position of chef at Nino's Place. "We mixed up too much disco with the food," he recalls in a marked French accent, "so I took off my toque and hung up my apron until I was asked to work here."

10 EMERSON PLACE
BOSTON

PETITE MARMITE HENRY IV

The broth for this soup is a demi-consommé so it must be very clear. Never let the soup boil rapidly or it will lose its lovely limpidity and go cloudy.

For the broth:

1 whole chicken
½ pound beef (from the top round)
1 onion, peeled and quartered, 1 quarter stuck with a clove
1 large carrot, peeled and coarsely chopped
1 stalk celery, coarsely chopped
Bouquet garni of bay leaf, thyme and parsley
20 peppercorns
2 teaspoons kosher salt
1 gallon water
Salt and pepper

For the garnish:

1 carrot, peeled and cut into matchsticks
1 turnip, peeled and cut into matchsticks
1 leek, white part only, washed and cut into matchsticks
¼ cup bone marrow (optional)
⅓ cup freshly grated Parmesan cheese
Sprigs of fresh chervil or chopped parsley

1. Place chicken, beef, onion, chopped carrot, celery, bouquet garni, peppercorns and kosher salt in a stock pot with water and bring just to the point of boiling. Skim stock, reduce heat and simmer for 1 to 1½ hours, skimming often to obtain a clear, well-flavored broth.
2. Strain the broth into a large saucepan, reserving chicken and beef, and boil until 1 quart liquid remains. Season with salt and pepper. Degrease with strips of paper towel.
3. Poach the vegetable matchsticks in the seasoned broth until tender, starting with the carrots and celery, which take the longest to cook.
4. Dice the beef and breast of the reserved chicken and add to the broth.
5. Thinly slice the marrow and poach in simmering soup for 30 seconds.
6. To serve, ladle into serving bowls. Sprinkle a spoonful of cheese in each bowl and garnish with chervil or parsley sprigs.

If it tastes good to you, it will taste good to your guests.

NOISETTES D'AGNEAU A LA DUCHESSE DE BERRY

1 (5- to 6-pound) saddle of lamb
Oil
2 cups chicken or veal stock (approximately)
1½ teaspoons tomato paste
6 tablespoons butter
2 tablespoons vermouth
Salt and pepper
Cooked Artichokes
Roast Cherry Tomatoes

1. Remove the lamb filets from the saddle, or have your butcher do it, and cut into 1½" steaks, called noisettes.
2. Make a "jus" with the lamb bones: chop bones into small pieces and brown darkly in oil. Add stock to cover and tomato paste; simmer 30 to 40 minutes to obtain ½ cup well-flavored jus.
3. Heat 3 tablespoons butter in a sauté pan and gently pan-fry the lamb noisettes for 3 minutes per side or until cooked to taste. (Lamb tastes best slightly pink in the center.) Transfer lamb to a platter and keep warm.
4. Heat the sauté pan and deglaze with vermouth, scraping with a wooden spatula to dissolve congealed meat juices. Strain the lamb jus into the pan and boil until reduced to about ¼ cup. Remove from heat and swirl in the remaining butter. Season to taste.
5. To serve the lamb, arrange the **Cooked Artichokes** around the noisettes and fill each with 3 **Roast Cherry Tomatoes**. Spoon a little sauce over each noisette and serve the remainder on the side.

A mechanic can tell his client that the car won't be ready until tomorrow. Not so a chef. The restaurant guest does not want to hear that the butcher came late, that the stove broke or that the dishwasher never showed up at work. The guest wants what he or she ordered 20 minutes after he or she ordered it and the chef had better produce, or else.

Cooked Artichokes

4 whole large artichokes
Lemon

1. Snap off the stems of the artichokes and cut off the top 1½". Snip off the points of the remaining leaves and use a spoon to scrape out the fibrous "choke" in the center. Rub the artichokes with lemon to prevent discoloration and squeeze lemon juice in the center.
2. Cook the artichokes in boiling, salted water for 30 minutes or until tender. Drain well before serving.

Roast Cherry Tomatoes

12 cherry tomatoes
2 tablespoons olive oil
Pinch of oregano
Salt and pepper

1. Preheat oven to 450°.
2. Place tomatoes in a small roasting pan and sprinkle with olive oil and seasonings. Roast for 10 minutes or until cooked.

The French don't seem to have much time for vegetables. In Italy, the vegetable is as important as the meat. Nouvelle cuisine has made such a fuss about leaving vegetables crispy. When I was growing up in Venice, my mother always served vegetables al dente.

SALADE TROPICALE

I developed this recipe when I was working in Florida. It is very refreshing after the main course and it helps clear the palate for dessert.

1 papaya, peeled, seeded and thinly sliced
1 avocado, peeled, seeded and thinly sliced
2 cups pimiento, thinly sliced
Juice of ½ lemon or to taste
1 tablespoon whiskey
Salt
2 fresh mint leaves, corsely chopped, plus 4 whole mint leaves
Sprigs of fresh chervil or parsley

Combine the fruits and vegetables in a salad bowl and toss with the flavorings, adding more lemon juice or salt as necessary. Arrange on chilled salad plates and garnish with whole mint leaves and parsley or chervil sprigs before serving.

SOUFFLE GLACE AU CITRON
Iced Lemon Soufflé

¾ cup sugar
3 egg yolks
Juice and grated rind of 2 lemons
2 cups heavy cream

1. Cook the sugar to the soft-ball stage (240° on a candy thermometer).
2. While sugar is cooking, place yolks in the bowl of a mixer and set speed on high for 2 minutes. Pour boiling sugar syrup in a thin stream over the yolks and continue beating until the mixture has completely cooled. Add the lemon juice and rind.
3. Whip the cream to semi-stiff peaks and gently fold into the yolk mixture, reserving a little cream for the decoration.
4. Spoon the soufflé mixture into a soufflé dish or individual ramekins or wine glasses and freeze for at least 5 hours. Decorate with whipped cream rosettes for serving.

A good maître d' has a sixth sense. His job is to foresee, predict, prevent, anticipate and read minds. When he talks with a client, his mind is busy discovering the client's food likes and dislikes, measuring his appetite, even counting the money in his pocket.

Panache

Dinner for Four

Warmed Scallops with Coriander

Sautéed Duck Panache

Green Beans with Garlic

Tangerine Mousse

Wine:

Corton-Charlemagne Diamond Jubilee
(Remoissenet Père et Fils) 1971

Bruce Frankel, Proprietor and Chef

Bruce Frankel did not set out to become the iconoclast of the Boston food scene, but his restaurant Panache has been at the center of controversy since it opened in January 1979. The young restaurateur baffled the critics with his unusual flavor combinations and small, nouvelle cuisine-sized portions. The public quickly recognized in Frankel, however, one of the most innovative and important of the Hub's new wave of chefs.

It's no accident people find a Zen-like quality in the Panache dining experience. For years Frankel adhered to a strict macrobiotic diet—a regimen of "controlled starvation," he recalls, which forced him to sharpen his culinary creativity. From there it was on to French cuisine, working at several Back Bay restaurants, where Frankel learned the classical foundations of cooking, plus an ever-evolving repertory of flavors and techniques. Oriental, European and American influences come together in Frankel's current creations—the fruits of what he calls a "highly stylized, highly personal cuisine."

The décor of Panache is a deliberate exercise in understatement and good taste. The name emblemizes the restaurant's élan perfectly, meaning "a plume of feathers" and by extension, anything with bravado, swagger and verve. It took bravado, indeed, to transform the dim Central Square storefront into the mecca of fine dining Panache is today.

"I guess I'm a radical in the truest sense of the word," says Frankel. "I'm trying to get to the roots of cooking. I've discarded all superfluities, like liveried waiters or garnishes you can't eat. I think that people would rather taste an interesting sauce, than one that is technically correct."

798 MAIN STREET
CAMBRIDGE

WARMED SCALLOPS WITH CORIANDER

This dish is an excellent example of nouvelle cuisine. It utilizes many of the "new" ingredients, a radical cooking technique, and a simple but striking presentation.

12 ounces fresh Bay or Cape scallops, half-moon-shaped muscle on
    the side of the scallops removed
3 branches fresh coriander
6 cups fish fumet (see index) or bottled clam juice
2 small shallots, very finely chopped
Salt to taste
12 coarse grinds of Szechuan peppercorns
1 tablespoon raspberry vinegar
1 tablespoon peanut oil
2 tablespoons walnut oil

1. Cut scallops horizontally into ¼" thick slices.
2. Pluck the coriander leaves from the stems, rinse in cold water, then dry between paper towels.
3. Slightly oversalt the fish fumet (but not the clam juice) and heat to a simmer.
4. Combine shallots, salt, Szechuan peppercorns and vinegar in a small mixing bowl and whisk in both oils drop by drop to obtain a rich emulsion. Taste and correct the seasoning.
5. Place scallops in a strainer and immerse in hot fish fumet for 30 seconds. Drain the scallops thoroughly on paper towels and divide evenly among 4 warm plates.
6. Sprinkle coriander leaves on top and pour the dressing over the scallops. Pat the scallops gently with your fingertips to mix in the dressing. Serve while still warm.

To me, nouvelle cuisine is the forefront of the evolution of cooking. No one is adding new dishes to Chinese or Hungarian cuisine. The French are regarded as the Establishment of the food world and yet they are coming out with this exciting new cuisine. Nouvelle cuisine is not some trendy little thing dreamed up by some bunch of kids; its advocates and pioneers are the most serious chefs in France.

SAUTEED DUCK PANACHE

*My sauces are stock reductions enriched with butter. I know of no
other way to achieve equal purity and concentration of flavor. This
is a higher level of sauce-making and it requires a lot of time and energy
to boil down the various ingredients. I think this is the direction sauces
have been pointing to over the last thirty years. . . . We go through
forty quarts of stock a day at Panache and the dining room seats forty.
That's what I mean by reduction cooking.*

2 whole, fresh 4- to 6-pound ducks
Salt and freshly ground white pepper to taste
Duck Stock
1 tablespoon granulated sugar
1 tablespoon sherry vinegar
¼ cup dry white wine
¼ teaspoon grated lemon rind
½ cup cold unsalted butter, cut into ¼" pieces

1. Use a sharp boning knife to remove the leg-thigh sections from each
   duck. Trim away all visible fat and all but a 1" border of skin and
   chop off the last ½" of the drumstick. Remove the breast halves
   from each duck by cutting along the breastbone and rib cage and
   trim all fat and sinewy membranes from the meat.
2. Preheat oven to 350°.
3. Place a large cast-iron frying pan over a medium flame and when
   the pan is hot, add the duck legs skin side down. Reduce heat.
   Salt and pepper the legs and fry for 10 minutes. Turn the legs and
   cook the meat side for only 3 minutes. Turn again and continue
   cooking until the skin is nicely browned and crispy.
4. Transfer the legs to a roasting pan and bake in preheated oven for
   30 minutes.
5. Meanwhile, place **Duck Stock** in a wide saucepan and boil until only
   1 cup liquid remains.
6. Place a small frying pan over a medium flame and when the pan is
   hot, sprinkle in the sugar. Cook sugar until it caramelizes, but do
   not let burn.
7. Remove caramel from heat and pour in the vinegar and wine to
   deglaze the pan. (Be careful: the mixture will sputter and sizzle.)
   You may need to stir the mixture with a whisk to completely
   dissolve the sugar.
8. Add the lemon rind and stock reduction. Simmer this mixture to
   obtain a consistency of light cream. Lower the heat and add the
   butter piece by piece, gently swirling the pan.

9. Correct the seasoning with salt and pepper, strain sauce through a fine sieve and reserve over warm water.

10. Remove duck legs from oven when done and pour off fat, reserving ¼". Cut legs at the joint and drain on paper towels. Keep warm.

11. Reheat the frying pan with the duck fat and cook the duck breasts 3 minutes per side for medium rare. Sprinkle with salt and pepper while cooking.

12. Pour the sauce onto 4 warm plates. Slice the duck breasts lengthwise and as thinly as possible and fan out the meat in the center of each plate. Arrange the thighs and drumsticks on either side of the duck breasts and serve at once.

Duck Stock

Carcasses, necks and giblets from the 2 ducks above
1 large onion, quartered
2 large carrots, coarsely chopped
2 ribs celery, chopped
2 cloves garlic, bruised
2 tablespoons tomato paste
Bouquet garni of bay leaf, thyme and parsley
20 black peppercorns
2 quarts cold water

1. Roast the duck carcasses in a hot oven until thoroughly browned.
   When bones begin to brown, add onion, carrots and celery and brown
   them as well.
2. Transfer the duck bones and vegetables to a large stockpot,
   discarding fat. Add the remaining ingredients. Bring the stock to
   a boil, skim and reduce heat to a simmer.
3. Simmer 3 to 5 hours, skimming from time to time to remove surface
   scum, adding cold water as necessary to end up with 7 cups of stock.
4. Strain and thoroughly degrease before using.

*Like most people who have opened restaurants, I tried a number of
times and failed before I opened Panache. The first try, you get so far
before you run into an obstacle you can't surmount. As you persist,
the obstacles get fewer and fewer. It took me ten years, but I finally
made it.*

GREEN BEANS WITH GARLIC

A woman once said, "I can't understand why Bruce Frankel is so successful. He doesn't even French his string beans!" It doesn't really matter if each little detail is perfect. I don't go around and measure each vegetable julienne with a micrometer. That woman will never know how to make a restaurant successful, because it has never occurred to her that the taste of the food matters more than how the green beans are cut.

1 pound green beans, washed and snapped
¼ cup unsalted butter
1 clove garlic, peeled and bruised
Salt and pepper

1. Cook the beans in at least 4 quarts of salted, boiling water for 3 minutes or to taste. They should remain a little crunchy. Remove beans and immerse immediately in ice-cold water. (This fixes the bright green color.)
2. Melt butter in a sauté pan and add the garlic and thoroughly drained green beans. Sauté to warm the beans and sprinkle with salt and pepper. Remove garlic and serve beans on a separate vegetable plate.

A good cook is a good cook. Either you are or you aren't. I think I have a talent for it. There is something special about me that comes out when I am cooking.

TANGERINE MOUSSE

Juice from 2 tangerines or enough to yield ½ cup
2 tablespoons fresh lemon juice
1½ teaspoons unflavored gelatin
3 eggs, separated
¼ cup plus 2 tablespoons sugar
1 cup heavy cream
Grated rind from 2 tangerines or enough to yield 1½ teaspoons
Pinch of salt
Tangerine Shells

1. Pour the tangerine and lemon juices over the gelatin and leave 15 minutes to soften.
2. Whisk the egg yolks with ¼ cup sugar for 5 minutes or until the mixture falls from the whisk or beater in a thick ribbon.
3. Set the yolk mixture over a pan of boiling water, reduce heat and stir constantly with a rubber spatula until the mixture becomes velvety and thickly coats the spatula.
4. Transfer the yolk mixture to a mixer and beat at a medium speed while warming the juice-gelatin mixture over boiling water. Add the juice-gelatin mixture to the yolk mixture, increasing mixer speed to fast. Beat until cool.
5. Beat the heavy cream with the grated tangerine rind to medium-stiff peaks. Fold into the cooled yolk mixture.
6. Beat the egg whites with a pinch of salt to medium-stiff peaks, beat in the remaining sugar and gently fold into mousse base. Chill 3 to 4 hours.
7. Just before serving, spoon the mousse generously into **Tangerine Shells**.

Tangerine Shells

1 egg white
½ cup sugar
1½ tablespoons clarified melted butter
Pinch of salt
1½ teaspoons grated tangerine rind
2½ tablespoons sifted flour

1. Combine the egg white, sugar, butter, salt and tangerine rind in a small mixing bowl.
2. Gradually whisk in the flour, beating until the mixture is free of lumps. Chill this batter for 1 hour.
3. Preheat the oven to 325° and butter and flour a large baking sheet.
4. Spoon the chilled batter onto the baking sheet in 6 drops, spreading each with the back of the spoon in a circular motion to form 6" rounds.
5. Bake the shells in preheated oven for 10 minutes or until golden brown. Carefully slide the shells off the baking sheet with a metal spatula and press over overturned teacups until cool.

I believe that the dining experience should be free from distractions. There are no useless garnishes on the plates at Panache. The service is discreet. I've kept the décor as simple and understated as possible.

RESTAURANT GENJI

Dinner for Six

Hamaguri-Siru
(Clam Soup)

Kaibashira-Sumiso
(Uncooked Marinated Scallops)

Tempura
(Batter-Fried Vegetables)

Sukiyaki
(Japanese Pan-Cooked Beef)

Ginger Ice Cream

Wine:

As an Apéritif—Plum Wine
With the Meal—Saki

Toshio Matsumoto, Owner
Nick Kobayashi, Chef

To cognoscenti of the Orient, the Genji were a royal family of twelfth-century Kyoto. To connoisseurs of Eastern cooking, Genji is a chic Japanese restaurant on Newbury Street. "I have tried to recreate the atmosphere of an imperial Japanese palace at my restaurant," says Genji owner Toshio Matsumoto. The costly misu screens and coffered ceilings, the elaborately carved Shinto shrine and the kimonoed waitresses lend the Restaurant Genji an air of royal majesty.

The Genji, which opened four years ago, offers two very different dining experiences. The downstairs specializes in kappo—Japan's classical cuisine—served in stunning Bento lacquerware. The upstairs features teppan—Japanese steakhouse dining—with swashbuckling chefs who cook right on the tables. Aficionados of vinegared rice and raw fish cakes line up at Genji's sushi bar for impeccably fresh sushi and sashimi. For the cross-legged crowd there's an authentic Japanese tearoom, with grass mats and a life-size tiger mural.

Tokyo-born Toshio Matsumoto brings extensive food experience to his restaurant. The son of a great Japanese restaurant family (his brother owns thirty restaurants in Tokyo), Matsumoto had several restaurants in New York prior to opening Genji. He sees himself as a culinary ambassador. "The Japanese consulate does not work very hard here, so I bring Oriental culture to the American people through the stomach," he says with a smile.

327 NEWBURY STREET
BOSTON

HAMAGURI-SIRU

12 cherrystone clams, thoroughly scrubbed
6 cups water
1 tablespoon saki
1 teaspoon salt
3 tablespoons dried bonito
6 paper-thin lemon slices
6 sprigs watercress

1. Place clams and water in a saucepan and simmer until clams open.
   Transfer clams with shells to 6 soup bowls, 2 clams per bowl.
2. Add the saki, salt and dried bonito to the clam broth and simmer
   very gently for 5 minutes. Strain the broth through a cheesecloth
   into the soup bowls.
3. Garnish each bowl with a lemon slice and sprig of watercress
   for serving.

Note: Saki is Japanese rice wine. Dried bonito, called katsuobushi, is
pre-flaked dried fish used for making fish stocks and flavoring sauces.
Both are available in most Oriental markets. Commercial fish or clam
base can be substituted for katsuobushi.

*The Japanese taste with their eyes as well as their palates. The visual
beauty of a dish is very important. Hungry people don't think about
taste or beauty. Once people are educated, they can appreciate the
beauty of a sauce or dish.*

KAIBASHIRA-SUMISO

¼ cup sugar
½ cup rice vinegar
2 egg yolks
½ cup saki
2 teaspoons Dijon-style mustard
1 cup miso
18 medium sea scallops, cut in half

Combine sugar, vinegar, egg yolks, saki, mustard and miso and stir in the scallops. Marinate at least 3 hours prior to serving.

Note: Miso is a strong, salty paste made from fermented soybeans. It is used to flavor soups and sauces. For this dish you should use shiro miso, which is lighter in color than aka miso. Because of its high salt content, miso will keep up to a year unrefrigerated even when opened.

The West should eat more seafood and more vegetables, like the Japanese. Too much meat makes people wild, gives them body odor, makes them lose their hair. I suggest that the American people eat more seaweed; it will keep them from growing bald.

TEMPURA

Tempura should be very, very crisp. The secret to good tempura lies in the batter; the water should be ice-cold when you add it.

1 medium-sized sweet potato, peeled and sliced into ¼" rounds
2 carrots, peeled and cut into ¼" strips
12 small asparagus stalks or 12 string beans, snapped
1 green pepper, seeded and cut into ¼" strips
12 large shrimp, shelled and deveined
3 eggs
1 cup flour
½ teaspoon baking powder
1 cup ice-cold water (approximately)
Dipping Sauce

1. Cut vegetables and arrange by kind with shrimp on a platter.
2. Beat the eggs in a bowl and sift in the flour and baking powder. Whisk the mixture, adding enough water to obtain a thin batter about the consistency of heavy cream.
3. Heat at least 2" of oil to 375° in a wide deep-frying pan or electric skillet. Using chopsticks or a fork, dip 1 piece of food at a time into the tempura batter and drop it into the oil. Fry ingredients of the same kind together, but do not overcrowd the pan.
4. Place tempura on paper towels to drain and serve at once with **Dipping Sauce**.

Dipping Sauce

2 teaspoons dried bonito
¼ cup boiling water
¼ cup mirin
¼ cup Japanese soy sauce

1. Add the bonito to boiling water and very gently simmer for 5 minutes.
2. Add mirin and soy sauce and strain. Sauce can be made ahead of time and should be served in small ramekins or little ceramic saucers.

Note: Mirin is sweet rice wine, sold in many Oriental grocery stores. While cream sherry is quite different, it makes a passible substitute. The **Dipping Sauce** can be made with fish or chicken stock instead of bonito and water, but the flavor, though tasty, will not be authentic.

Japanese soy sauce is superior because we use fermented rice to make it. It contains a certain kind of bacteria, like penicillin, which is good for the body. It has a nice taste too—slightly sweet.

SUKIYAKI

Chef Nick Kobayashi agreed to include Genji's famous teriyaki in his menu for Dining In—Boston. *When I asked him to give me the recipe, however, he told me to write down six letters: S-E-C-R-E-T. Below he reveals the recipe for that other Japanese beef classic—sukiyaki.*

1½ to 2 pounds beef sirloin, shaved into ⅛" thick slices (choose a piece of beef with some fat on it—you'll need 2 to 3 cubes of fat to grease the frying pan)
1 can agar-agar noodles
2 onions, very thinly sliced
1 bunch watercress, thick stems removed
12 ounces fresh spinach, washed and stems removed
1 (12-ounce) package mushrooms, washed and thinly sliced
¼ cup soy sauce
2 tablespoons sugar
2 tablespoons saki
2 tablespoons mirin
2 tablespoons water

1. Heat a large skillet or electric frying pan and add beef fat. Push the cubes around with chopsticks to thoroughly coat the pan with melted fat and then remove.
2. Arrange the meat, noodles and vegetables on a platter.
3. Combine soy sauce, sugar, saki, mirin and water.
4. Add half the meat, noodles and vegetables to the hot pan, keeping each ingredient separate. Fry each until tender, but do not overcook the vegetables.
5. Pour half the sauce over the sukiyaki and wait until it begins to sizzle.
6. Serve at once. Cook the remaining ingredients the same way.

Note: Agar-agar noodles are made from gelatin-rich seaweed. They are available canned in most Oriental grocery stores.

Sukiyaki is usually prepared right at the table in Japan. The tables in Genji's teppan rooms have special heated surfaces for cooking sukiyaki and teriyaki in front of our guests. You can use an electric frying pan or hot plate and skillet when preparing sukiyaki at the table at home.

GINGER ICE CREAM

1½ pints homemade or good commercial vanilla ice cream
6 tablespoons coarsely chopped candied ginger (approximately)

1. Soften the ice cream with a wooden spoon and stir in the ginger to taste.
2. Return to the freezer to harden for at least 2 hours prior to serving.

The Voyagers

Dinner for Six

Turban of Salmon, Sole and Spinach

Chicken Aficionado

Honey-Lemon Carrots

Green and Gold Squash

Strawberries Cassis

Wine:

With Fish—Charles Heidsieck Brut Champagne 1973
With Chicken—Château Brane-Cantenac 1966
With Dessert—Piesporter Goldtröpfchen Riesling
Auslese 1976

Dorothy Koval, Chef

The Voyagers restaurant near Harvard Square may be the only eating establishment in Boston where guests can dine under the stars in a rooftop greenhouse surrounded by lush foliage and murmuring fountains. Then again, few restaurants pamper their clients with calligraphic place cards, hand-blown stemware and nightly concerts of live harp and harpsichord music. It is rare in this day to find a restaurant which attends to such a multitude of details. At the Voyagers, guests are continually reminded how much the setting, ambience, music, tableware and service of a restaurant enhance the cuisine.

The three dining rooms at the Voyagers feature revolving exhibits of contemporary and Oriental art, plus prints of the Old Masters. A handsome newsletter keeps patrons abreast of the latest expositions. It is no accident that the visual arts and music figure prominently in the dining experience at the Voyagers. Chef Dorothy Koval gave up a career as an art gallery director three years ago to take charge of the Voyagers kitchen.

"I had never had any restaurant experience before the Voyagers," recalls Chef Koval with a smile. "The freedom from the prejudices of the professional, however, has proved much more a benefit than a handicap." Koval describes her cooking as a personal cuisine which changes seasonally. She leans toward the specialties of France and Italy to a point and then her imagination takes over.

The entire staff at the Voyagers sees cooking as a total experience which begins in the garden and ends in the dining room. The cooks grow their own herbs, make their own vinegar, smoke their own quail. Unlike most restaurants, at the Voyagers the waiters often lend a hand in the kitchen. The service is well informed, but informal.

45½ MT. AUBURN STREET
CAMBRIDGE

TURBAN OF SALMON, SOLE AND SPINACH

2 pounds spinach, washed and stems removed
2 tablespoons minced shallots
¼ cup butter
Salt and pepper
Freshly grated nutmeg
Juice of ½ lemon
2 pounds fresh salmon, boned, skinned and diced
Dash of Tabasco sauce
2 eggs
2 pints medium cream
2 pounds thin, flat filets of sole
Lettuce leaves
Lemon wedges
Radishes

1. Cook the spinach in boiling, salted water until limp and drain. Squeeze spinach to wring out all the water and chop finely.
2. Lightly sauté the shallots in butter. Add the spinach, increase heat to high and cook for 3 to 5 minutes to evaporate excess moisture. Season with salt, pepper, nutmeg and lemon juice. Set aside.
3. Purée half the salmon in a food processor and gradually incorporate salt, nutmeg, Tabasco sauce, 1 egg and 1 pint cream. Process until the mixture is smooth. Repeat the procedure with the remaining salmon, egg and cream. Combine the salmon mixtures and chill.
4. Preheat the oven to 350°. Bring 3" water to a boil in a roasting pan.
5. Generously butter a 6-cup ring mold and line with the sole filets.
6. Divide the salmon mixture in thirds and spoon the first part into the mold over the sole. Place half the spinach on top of the salmon mixture, add another third of the salmon, the remaining spinach, then the remaining salmon.
7. Cover with buttered waxed paper and a double layer of aluminum foil, set mold in prepared pan of boiling water and bake in preheated oven for 50 to 60 minutes or until the turban feels firm to the touch.
8. Remove from oven, take off foil and allow to cool before unmolding onto a plate somewhat larger than the mold. Drain the turban thoroughly and refrigerate for several hours or overnight.
9. To serve, slice the turban and arrange on plates lined with lettuce leaves. Garnish with lemon wedges and radishes.

CHICKEN AFICIONADO

6 chicken breasts, boned and split
6 tablespoons butter (or more as necessary)
Salt and pepper
1 tablespoon minced shallots
¼ pound thinly sliced Prosciutto ham, cut into thin slivers
¼ pound mushrooms, washed and thinly sliced
½ to ¾ pound chicken livers, each cut in quarters
Flour for dusting
Pinch of thyme
1 cup Madeira
¼ cup butter

1. Pound the chicken breasts between 2 pieces of waxed paper until about ⅓" thick.
2. Melt the butter in 2 skillets and heat over a moderate flame until foamy. Add the chicken and sauté both sides for a few minutes until the flesh turns opaque. Remove chicken from pan, season lightly with salt and pepper and transfer to a warm platter.
3. Increase heat to high, adding more butter to pans if necessary, and add the shallots, Prosciutto and mushrooms. Dust the chicken livers with flour and add to pan with salt, pepper and thyme. Sauté until the chicken livers are nicely browned, shaking the pan to prevent sticking.
4. Pour ½ cup Madeira into each pan and deglaze, scraping with a wooden spatula to dissolve congealed meat juices.
5. Transfer the Prosciutto, mushrooms and chicken livers to the chicken platter with a slotted spoon.
6. Combine the juices in 1 pan and boil until thick and syrupy—approximately ½ cup should remain. Swirl in the remaining butter and pour sauce over the chicken. Serve at once.

We have always felt that the perfect complement to fine food is carefully selected wine. We decant all of our red wines, unless they have no sediment. Our white wines are not stored under refrigeration, but chilled in ice on serving.

It's hard to know how much to put into a recipe. You want to give people plenty of freedom to cook to their own taste.

My advice to the neophyte is this: you can do a lot more than you think you can, if only you can survive the first two months in the restaurant.

HONEY-LEMON CARROTS

3 pounds carrots, peeled and cut into sticks
2 bunches scallions, tops and roots trimmed
6 tablespoons melted butter
¾ teaspoon salt
3 tablespoons honey
Juice and grated rind of 1 lemon

1. Immerse the carrots and scallions in boiling, well-salted water and cook until tender crisp. Place in cold water to stop cooking and drain.
2. Preheat oven to 350°.
3. Combine the remaining ingredients, varying the proportions according to the sweetness of the carrots. Place carrots and scallions in a baking dish, pour the sauce over them and bake for 15 minutes.

To me it is very important to have a connection with the whole food process, from garden, to kitchen, to table. We grow many of our own herbs and vegetables. Our serving people often help out in the kitchen.

GREEN AND GOLD SQUASH

The fresher a vegetable, the more quickly it cooks. We try to use as much organically grown produce as possible. It tastes better and cooks more rapidly because it's not all bound up in cellulose.

3 small zucchini
3 small summer or yellow squash
Salt
1 tablespoon chopped shallots
¼ cup softened butter
Freshly ground black pepper

1. Wash and thinly slice the squash.
2. Bring ½" water to a boil in a wide sauté pan with salt and shallots. Add the squash, cover pan and steam for 2 to 3 minutes or until tender.
3. Pour off the water and toss the squash with butter and pepper. Serve at once.

STRAWBERRIES CASSIS

1 cup **Crème Fraîche**
¾ cup heavy cream, stiffly whipped
¼ cup crème de cassis
Splash of port wine
Squeeze of lemon juice
Sugar to taste
2 quarts fresh ripe strawberries, washed and hulled
1 cup seedless grapes
3 tablespoons shelled, chopped pistachio nuts

1. Combine **Crème Fraîche**, whipped cream, crème de cassis, port, lemon juice and sugar, adjusting the sweetness or tartness to suit the berries.
2. Arrange the berries and grapes in a glass bowl and pour the sauce over them, letting some of the bright red peek out. Garnish with chopped pistachio nuts for serving.

Note: Crème de cassis is a liqueur made from black currants. It is available in specialty spirit shops.

Crème Fraîche

This recipe makes five cups. The extra will keep in the refrigerator for up to two weeks.

1 quart heavy cream
1 pint buttermilk or sour cream

Combine the cream and buttermilk and heat to tepid. Cover and let stand in a warm place overnight. When the mixture is thick and sourish, the **Crème Fraîche** is ready.

This recipe produces a good approximation of the thick, sourish cream used by the French.

We try to emphasize knowledge, rather than formality, in our service.

As a self-taught cook, I have much more freedom than someone who was trained at cooking school. I haven't been told what I must or must not do.

ZACHARY'S
THE COLONNADE HOTEL

Dinner for Six

Casserole Rockefeller

Green Bean Salad

Truite à la Muscovite

Pommes Persil

Gâteau Colonnade

Wine:

*With Scallops and Trout—Corton-Charlemagne
(Louis Latour) 1973
With Dessert—Château d'Yquem 1971*

Victor Pap, Chef

Nine short years after the opening of the Colonnade Hotel a few blocks west of Copley Square, its luxury restaurant, Zachary's, has won national acclaim for its Continental cuisine and formal French service. Recipient of a distinguished restaurant award from United Airline's *Mainliner* magazine, Zachary's has hosted dinners for prestigious gourmet societies such as the Chaîne de Rôtisseurs and Les Amis d'Escoffier. Colonnade guests have included Beverly Sills, Ryan O'Neal, Golda Meir and former President Ford.

It is easy to see why the Colonnade prides itself on Zachary's unique setting. The dining room is a facsimile of the famous French cruise ship *Degrasse*, which plied the seas in the 1920s and '30s. Antique French chrome mirrors and custom fabrics adorn the walls of the 115-seat dining area. Zachary's guests dine on fine Rosenthal china imported from Germany.

Zachary's bill of fare reflects the international background of Executive Chef Victor Pap. Born in Hungary, the thirty-two-year-old chef trained in Austria, Italy and Germany, before coming to Boston four years ago. A three-year veteran at Zachary's, Pap oversees thirteen chefs and a four-man pastry team who help him add sixty new dishes to Zachary's menu each year.

Pap's counterpart in the dining room is third-generation maître d', Paolo Zappala. When it comes to flambéing, salad spinning and duck carving, few can surpass his aplomb. One evening a gentleman asked Zappala to help him surprise a lady friend. The mustachioed maître d' readily obliged by placing a diamond ring inside a whipped-cream pastry.

120 HUNTINGTON AVENUE
BOSTON

CASSEROLE ROCKEFELLER

½ cup butter
3 pounds spinach, thoroughly washed and stems removed
¼ cup Pernod or other anise-flavored liqueur
6 tablespoons **White Sauce**
Salt and pepper
1½ pounds Bay or Cape scallops
1 cup dried bread crumbs

1. Melt 3 tablespoons butter in a large sauté pan and cook the spinach with Pernod. Once the leaves wilt, increase heat to evaporate excess moisture. Remove from heat and set aside.
2. Chop spinach coarsely, stir in the **White Sauce** and correct the seasoning.
3. Butter 6 small ramekins or scallop shells and divide the mixture among them.
4. Preheat oven to 500°.
5. Season the scallops with salt and pepper and dredge in bread crumbs, shaking off excess. Place on top of spinach.
6. Dot with the remaining butter and bake in preheated oven until golden brown—approximately 6 to 8 minutes. Serve immediately.

White Sauce

2 teaspoons butter
2 teaspoons flour
⅓ cup milk
Grate of fresh nutmeg
Salt and pepper

Melt the butter in a small saucepan and whisk in the flour. Cook for 3 minutes, but do not let brown. Gradually whisk in the milk and simmer for 3 more minutes. Season to taste before using.

Why do we change our menu only once a year? I can only quote from Goethe: "Art is long; life, short." At Zachary's, we prepare cuisine which is a work of art.

GREEN BEAN SALAD

1½ pounds green beans, washed, snapped and sliced on the diagonal
⅓ cup red wine vinegar
3 tablespoons olive oil
1 small onion, finely chopped
½ teaspoon salt
¼ teaspoon freshly ground black pepper
Lettuce leaves
Diced pimiento

1. Immerse the green beans in a large pot of boiling, salted water and cook for 3 to 4 minutes or until tender crisp. Drain.
2. Combine the vinegar, oil, onion, salt and pepper and add the hot green beans. Chill for at least 1 hour.
3. Arrange lettuce leaves on 6 chilled salad plates. Drain green beans and pile in the center. Garnish with diced pimiento before serving.

Think of Zachary's as Symphony Hall and the chef as the composer. The maître d' plays the role of the conductor, ensuring that the guests are served the food properly and that the performance unfolds in the dining room exactly as it was conceived by the chef in the kitchen.

TRUITE A LA MUSCOVITE

6 (10-ounce) trout
¾ cup chopped onion
6 tablespoons butter
3 tablespoons flour
9 ounces cooked lump crab meat, picked over and flaked
1½ tablespoons Salignac or other fine Cognac
1½ tablespoons black caviar
2 teaspoons finely chopped parsley
¼ teaspoon chervil
Salt and pepper
1 egg plus 1 yolk, beaten
Flour for dredging
½ cup olive oil
Caviar Sauce
Parsley sprigs
Lemon wedges

1. Clean trout through the gills and remove backbones, leaving the heads and tails intact (or have your fishmonger do it). Rinse and pat dry.
2. Briskly sauté onion in butter for 3 minutes or until golden. Stir in the flour and cook for 1 minute. Add the crab meat, Cognac, caviar, parsley, chervil, salt and pepper and cook to heat the mixture through. Stir in the egg and yolk and cook for 1 minute. Remove from heat and let cool.
3. Preheat oven to 350°.
4. Season the trout cavities with salt and pepper. Spread the trout open, divide the stuffing evenly among the cavities and press closed.
5. Dredge trout in flour, shaking off excess, and sauté over high heat in a large skillet in olive oil for 2 minutes per side.
6. Transfer to an oven-proof platter and bake for 12 to 15 minutes. Arrange on a serving platter and spoon the **Caviar Sauce** on top. Garnish with parsley sprigs and lemon wedges for serving.

Caviar Sauce

6 tablespoons butter (clarified if possible)
6 tablespoons flour
2¼ cups fish stock (see index) or bottled clam juice
½ cup sour cream
¼ cup dry white wine
Pinch of thyme
Salt and pepper
3 tablespoons caviar
1½ tablespoons butter

1. Melt butter in a saucepan and whisk in the flour. Cook for 3 minutes or until golden. Gradually whisk in the fish stock and simmer, stirring for 5 minutes. Add sour cream, wine and seasonings and simmer for 5 more minutes.
2. Strain sauce and gently stir in the caviar. Dot with butter to prevent a skin from forming. Keep warm.

Perfection requires enormous planning and practice. Great dishes are not born overnight.

POMMES PERSIL

6 boiling potatoes, peeled and quartered
3 tablespoons butter
3 tablespoons finely chopped parsley

Place the potatoes in a large pot with ½" salted water. Bring to a boil, cover pan and steam potatoes 25 minutes or until tender. Place in a serving dish and toss with butter and parsley.

GATEAU COLONNADE

1 cup sugar
⅓ cup cocoa
¾ cup cake flour
1 cup milk
½ cup unsalted butter at room temperature
1 teaspoon baking powder
1 teaspoon baking soda
6 eggs
Chocolate Mint Frosting

1. Preheat oven to 350°.
2. Grease and lightly flour 3 (8") cake pans and line the bottoms with waxed paper.
3. Combine the sugar, cocoa, flour and ⅓ cup milk in the bowl of a mixer. Beat in the butter, baking powder and baking soda, mixing at medium speed for 5 minutes.
4. Beat in 3 eggs and 3 tablespoons milk. Continue mixing for 2 to 3 minutes, scraping sides and bottom of bowl frequently. Add the remaining eggs and milk. Beat at high speed for 1 minute.
5. Pour batter into prepared pans and bake in preheated oven for 20 minutes or until the tops spring back when pressed gently. Cool and turn out onto a wire rack. Be sure to remove the waxed paper.
6. Ice each cake with **Chocolate Mint Frosting** and stack the layers. Smooth the icing on top with a spatula. This cake serves 12 to 14.

Chocolate Mint Frosting

¼ cup milk
8 ounces unsweetened chocolate
¾ cup confectioners' sugar
⅙ cup white corn syrup
2 tablespoons crème de menthe

Combine milk, chocolate, sugar and corn syrup in a saucepan and bring barely to a boil, stirring constantly. Cool and stir in the liqueur.

The Gâteau Colonnade is probably our most famous dessert. The critics say it's the best chocolate cake in Boston.

INDEX

Desserts and Dessert Accents

Entrées

Pastas

Salad Dressings

Salads

Sauces and Special Seasonings

Soups and Stocks

Sorbet

Vegetables and Side Dishes

DINING IN—THE GREAT CITIES

A Collection of Gourmet Recipes from the Finest Chefs in the Country

If you enjoyed **Dining In—Boston**, the following
cookbook/restaurant guides are now available:

___ Dining In—Boston
___ Dining In—Chicago
___ Dining In—Dallas
___ Dining In—Houston, Vol. I
___ Dining In—Houston, Vol. II
___ Dining In—Los Angeles
___ Dining In—Minneapolis/St. Paul
___ Dining In—Monterey Peninsula
___ Dining In—Pittsburgh

___ Dining In—Portland
___ Dining In—St. Louis
___ Dining In—San Francisco
___ Dining In—Seattle, Vol. I
___ Dining In—Seattle, Vol. II
___ Dining In—Toronto

___ Feasting In—Atlanta
___ Feasting In—New Orleans

Forthcoming Titles:

___ Dining In—Baltimore
___ Dining In—Honolulu/Maui
___ Dining In—Kansas City

___ Dining In—Philadelphia
___ Dining In—San Diego

To order, send $7.95 plus $1.00 postage and handling for each book.

> ☐ CHECK HERE IF YOU WOULD LIKE TO HAVE A
> DIFFERENT **DINING IN** COOKBOOK SENT TO YOU
> ONCE A MONTH.
> Payable by Mastercard, Visa or COD. Returnable if not satisfied
> $7.95 plus $1.00 postage and handling for each book

. . . .

BILL TO:

Name _____

Address _____

City_____ State_____ Zip _____

☐ Payment enclosed   ☐ Send COD

☐ Charge

Visa # _____

Exp. Date_____

Mastercard # _____

Exp. Date _____

Signature_____

SHIP TO:

Name _____

Address _____

City_____ State_____ Zip _____

. . . .

Name_____

Address_____

City_____ State _____ Zip_____

. . . .

Name_____

Address_____

City_____ State _____ Zip_____

PEANUT BUTTER PUBLISHING

PEANUT BUTTER TOWERS · 2733 4TH AVENUE SOUTH · SEATTLE, WA 98134